THE CHURCH CAT

Other short-story collections edited by Mark Bryant

CAT TALES FOR CHRISTMAS
COUNTRY TALES FOR CHRISTMAS
CHILDHOOD TALES FOR CHRISTMAS
SINS OF THE FATHERS

The Church Cat

Clerical Cats in Stories and Verse

Edited by Mark Bryant

Hodder & Stoughton

LONDON   SYDNEY   AUCKLAND

Introduction and collection copyright © 1997
by Mark Bryant

First published in Great Britain in 1997

The right of Mark Bryant to be identified as the Editor of
the Work has been asserted by him in accordance with the
Copyright, Designs and Patents Act 1988.

3 5 7 9 10 8 6 4 2

A CIP catalogue record for this title is available
from the British Library

ISBN 0 340 69423 8 [hardback edition]
ISBN 0 340 69424 6 [paperback edition]

Typeset by Palimpsest Book Production Limited,
Polmont, Stirlingshire
Printed and bound in Great Britain by
Mackays of Chatham PLC, Chatham, Kent

Hodder and Stoughton
A division of Hodder Headline PLC
338 Euston Road
London NW1 3BH

For my mother,
Dena Bryant

Contents

Introduction

A smudge-black shadow disappears through the lych-gate.
Green eyes glimmer from a stone-sealed tomb. High up
in the belfry an inhuman cry echoes . . . A ghost? Perhaps.
More likely the churchyard cat.

Cats and the clergy are natural soulmates. Whether
it's the bishop's tabby or the sexton's Siamese, cats and
churches have long been inseparable. And, indeed, some
have even detected an instinctive clerical bearing in the
feline mentality itself. The philosopher Jeremy Bentham's
macaroni-eating cat, the Rev. Sir John Langbourne, was
generally agreed to be 'not far off a mitre' when he died,
and Carl van Vechten, author of the celebrated book *The
Tiger in the House*, declared that 'Cats have gnosis to a degree
that is granted to few bishops.' Yet, curiously enough, there
is not a single mention of cats in the Bible, and they are
noticeably absent in Noah's Ark. However, one tradition
has it that there was a cat in the stable during the birth
of Jesus and that the 'M'-shaped fur pattern between the
ears on a tabby's head derives from when the Virgin Mary
gently pushed the inquisitive puss away from the new-born
Saviour.

In Ancient Egypt, of course, the cat was revered, and
in more recent times the ecclesiastical cat has become
a common sight. As well as numerous lesser clergy, no
fewer than three popes are recorded as having kept them

as pets, and Cardinal Richelieu himself reputedly owned fourteen – and left a sizeable pension to each in his will. Another cardinal, Thomas Wolsey, always had his black cat beside him when pronouncing judgments of state. Carved feline effigies also frequently appear on choirstalls both in Britain and overseas. And some church cats have even had monuments erected to their memory, such as that to Tommy in St Mary's, Redcliffe, Bristol, while Ginge of Salisbury Cathedral not only has his own gravestone but also features in a stained-glass window.

Thus it will come as no surprise to learn that clerical cats have also inspired some of the best works of modern literary fiction. This book is a collection of some of these stories and poems about cats and churches, covering every aspect of ecclesiastical life, and includes contributions by a priest, a Wesleyan Methodist minister, a biblical scholar, a religious poet, a hymn writer and the daughter of the prebendary of Lichfield, among others. I have tried to make the anthology as balanced as the limitations of length and copyright availability have allowed; it contains work by both men and women from the eighteenth century up to the present day and a variety of genres, from crime and romance to horror and humour, some of which is published here for the very first time.

So whether you are a Christian or agnostic, priest or layman, settle down in your favourite armchair by the window as dusk creeps over the churchyard and the birds start to yawn in the gnarled old oak. Then, as the last peal fades from the clocktower and a familiar black shape slips once more through the lych-gate, drift off into a world of clerical cats, of stories and verse macabre and cosy, sentimental and strange . . .

Mark Bryant

Abner of the Porch

Geoffrey Household

When my voice broke, even Abner and MacGillivray understood my grief. I did not expect sympathy from MacGillivray, for he had no reason to like me. But he knew what it was to be excluded from cathedral ceremonies. He was the bishop's dog.

Abner was masterless. I would not claim that he appreciated the alto's solo in the *Magnificat* when the organ was hushed and there was no other sound in the million and a half cubic feet of the cathedral but the slender purity of a boy's voice; yet he would patronise me after such occasions with the air of the master alto which he might have been. Though not a full tom, he knew the ancestral songs which resemble our own. To our ears the scale of cats is distasteful, but one cannot deny them sustained notes of singular loveliness and clarity.

Abner's career had followed a common human pattern. My father was the gardener, responsible for the shaven lawns and discreet flower-beds of the cathedral close. Some three years earlier he had suffered from an invasion of moles – creatures of ecclesiastical subtlety who avoided all the crude traps set for them by a mere layman. The cat, appearing from nowhere, took an interest. After a week he had caught the lot, laying out his game-bag each morning upon the tarpaulin which covered the mower.

Fed and praised by my father, he began to pay some attention to public relations and attracted the attention of visitors. Officially recognised as an ornament of the cathedral when his photograph appeared in the local paper, he ventured to advance from the lawns and tombstones to the porch. There he captivated the dean, always politely rising from the stone bench and thrusting his noble flanks against the gaitered leg. He was most gracious to the bishop and the higher clergy, but he would only stroke the dean. He knew very well from bearing and tone of voice, gentle though they were, that the cathedral belonged to him. It was the dean who christened him Abner.

To such a personage the dog of our new bishop was a disaster. MacGillivray was of respectable middle age, and had on occasion a sense of dignity; but when dignity was not called for he behaved like any other Aberdeen terrier and would race joyously round the cathedral or across the close, defying whatever human being was in charge of him to catch the lead which bounced and flew behind.

His first meeting with his rival set the future tone of their relations. He ventured with appalling temerity to make sport of the cathedral cat. Abner stretched himself, yawned, allowed MacGillivray's charge to approach within a yard, leaped to the narrow and rounded top of a tombstone and, draping himself over it, went ostentatiously to sleep. MacGillivray jumped and yapped at the tail tip which graciously waved for him, and then realised that he was being treated as a puppy. After that, the two passed each other politely but without remark. In our closed world of the cathedral such coolness between servants of dean and servants of bishop was familiar.

MacGillivray considered that he should be on permanent

duty with his master. Since he was black, small and ingenious, it was difficult to prevent him. So devoted a friend could not be cruelly chained – and in summer the french windows of the Bishop's Palace were always open.

He first endeared himself to choir and clergy at the ceremony of the bishop's installation. Magnificent in mitre and full robes, the bishop at the head of his procession knocked with his crozier upon the cathedral door to demand admission. MacGillivray, observing that his master was shut out and in need of help, hurtled across the close, bounced at the door and added his excited barks to the formal solemnity of the bishop's order.

Led away in disapproving silence, he took the enormity of his crime more seriously than we did. On his next appearance he behaved with decent humility, following the unconscious bishop down the chancel and into the pulpit with bowed head and tail well below horizontal.

Such anxious piety was even more embarrassing than bounce. It became my duty, laid upon me by the bishop in person, to ensure on all formal occasions that MacGillivray had not evaded the butler and was safely confined. I was even empowered to tie him up to the railings on the north side of the close in cases of emergency.

I do not think the bishop ever realised what was troubling his friend and erring brother, MacGillivray – normally a dog of sense who could mind his own business however great his affection for his master. When he accompanied the bishop around the diocese he never committed the solecism of entering a parish church and never used the vicar's cat as an objective for assault practice.

His indiscipline at home was, we were all sure, due to jealousy of Abner. He resented with Scottish obstinacy the fact that he was ejected in disgrace from the cathedral whereas Abner was not. He could not be expected to understand that Abner's discreet movements were beyond human control.

The dean could and did quite honestly declare that he had never seen that cat in the cathedral. Younger eyes, however, which knew where to look, had often distinguished Abner curled up on the ornate stone canopy over the tomb of a seventeenth-century admiral. In winter, he would sometimes sleep upon the left arm of a stone crusader in the cavity between shield and mailed shirt – a dank spot, I thought, until I discovered that it captured a current of warm air from the grating beside the effigy. In both his resting-places he was, if he chose to be, invisible. He was half Persian, tiger-striped with brownish grey on lighter grey, and he matched the stone of the cathedral.

As the summer went by, the feud between Abner and MacGillivray became more subtle. Both scored points. MacGillivray, if he woke up feeling youthful, used to chase the tame pigeons in the close. One morning, to the surprise of both dog and bird, a pigeon failed to get out of the way in time and broke a wing. MacGillivray was embarrassed. He sniffed the pigeon, wagged his tail to show that there was no ill-feeling and sat down to think.

Abner strolled from the porch and held down the pigeon with a firm, gentle paw. He picked it up in his mouth and presented it with liquid and appealing eyes to an elegant American tourist who was musing sentimentally in the close. She swore that the cat had asked her to heal the bird – which, by remaining a whole week in our town in and out of the vet's consulting room, she did. Personally, I think that Abner was attracted by the feline grace of her walk and was suggesting that, as the pigeon could be of no more use to the cathedral, she might as well eat it. But whatever his motives, he had again made MacGillivray look a clumsy and impulsive fool.

MacGillivray's revenge was a little primitive. He deposited bones and offal in dark corners of the porch and pretended that Abner had put them there. That was the second worst crime he knew – to leave on a human floor the inedible portion of his meals.

The verger was deceived and submitted a grave complaint in writing to the dean. The dean, however, knew very well that Abner had no interest in mutton bones, old or new. He was familiar with the cat's tastes. Indeed, it was rumoured from the deanery that he secreted a little box in his pocket at meals, into which he would drop such delicacies as the head of a small trout or the liver of a roast duck.

I cannot remember all the incidents of the cold war. And, anyway, I could not swear to their truth. My father and the dean read into the animals' behaviour motives which were highly unlikely and then shamelessly embroidered them, creating a whole miscellany of private legend for the canons and the choir. So I will only repeat the triumph of MacGillivray and its sequel, both of which I saw myself.

That fulfilment of every dog's dream appeared at first final and overwhelming victory. It was 1 September, the feast of St Giles, our patron saint. Evensong was a full choral and instrumental service, traditional, exquisite, and attracting a congregation whose interest was in music rather than religion. The bishop was to preach. Perhaps the effort of composition, of appealing to well-read intellectuals without offending the simpler clergy, had created an atmosphere of hard work and anxiety in the bishop's study. At any rate, MacGillivray was nervous and mischievous.

While I was ensuring his comfort before shutting him up, he twitched the lead out of my hand and was off on his quarter-mile course round the cathedral looking for a private entrance. When at last I caught him, the changes of the bells had stopped. I had only five minutes before the processional entry of the choir. There wasn't even time to race across the close and tie him up to the railings.

I rushed into the north transept with MacGillivray under my arm, pushed him down the stairs into the crypt and shut the door behind him. I knew that he could not get out. Our Norman crypt was closed to visitors during the service, and no one on a summer evening would have reason to go down to the masons' and carpenters' stores, the strong-room or the boilers. All I feared was that MacGillivray's yaps might be heard through the gratings in the cathedral floor.

I dived into my ruffled surplice and took my place in the procession, earning the blackest possible looks from the choir-master. I just had time to explain to him that it was the fault of MacGillivray. I was not forgiven, but the grin exchanged between choir-master and precentor suggested that I probably would be – if I wasn't still panting by the time that the alto had to praise all famous men and our fathers that begat us.

St Giles, if he still had any taste for earthly music, must have approved his servants that evening. The bishop, always an effective preacher, surpassed himself. His sinewy arguments were of course beyond me, but I had my eye – vain little beast that I was – on the music critics from the London papers, and I could see that several of them were so interested that they were bursting to take over the pulpit and reply.

Only once did he falter, when the barking of MacGillivray, hardly perceptible to anyone but his master and me, caught the episcopal ear. Even then his momentary hesitation was put down to a search for the right word.

I felt that my desperate disposal of MacGillivray might

not be appreciated. He must have been audible to any of the congregation sitting near the gratings of the northern aisle. So I shot down to release him immediately after the recessional. The noise was startling as soon as I opened the door. MacGillivray was holding the stairs against a stranger in the crypt.

The man was good-dogging him and trying to make him shut up. He had a small suitcase by his side. When two sturdy vergers, attracted by the noise, appeared hot on my heels, the intruder tried to bolt – dragging behind him MacGillivray with teeth closed on the turn-ups of his trousers. We detained him and opened the suitcase. It contained twenty pounds' weight of the cathedral silver. During the long service our massive but primitive strong-room door had been expertly opened.

The congregation was dispersing, but bishop, dean, archdeacon and innumerable canons were still in the cathedral. They attended the excitement just as any other crowd. Under the circumstances, MacGillivray was the centre of the most complimentary fuss. The canons would have genially petted any dog. But this was the bishop's dog. The wings of gowns and surplices flowed over him like those of exclamatory seagulls descending upon a stranded fish.

Dignity was represented only by our local superintendent of police and the terrier himself. When the thief had been led away, MacGillivray reverently followed his master out of the cathedral; his whole attitude reproached us for ever dreaming that he might take advantage of his popularity.

At the porch, however, he turned round and loosed one short, triumphant bark into the empty nave. The bishop's chaplain unctuously suggested that it was a little voice of thanksgiving. So it was – but far from pious. I noticed where MacGillivray's muzzle was pointing. That bark was

7

for a softness of outline, a shadow, a striping of small stone pinnacles upon the canopy of the Admiral's Tomb.

For several days – all of ten I should say – Abner deserted both the cathedral and its porch. He then returned to his first friend, helping my father to make the last autumn cut of the grass and offering his catch of small game for approval. The dean suggested that he was in need of sunshine. My father shook his head and said nothing. It was obvious to both of us that for Abner the cathedral had been momentarily defiled. He reminded me of an old verger who gave in his resignation – it was long overdue anyway – after discovering a family party eating lunch from paper bags in the Lady Chapel.

He went back to the porch a little before the harvest festival, for he always enjoyed that. During a whole week while the decorations were in place he could find a number of discreet lairs where it was impossible to detect his presence. There may also have been a little hunting in the night. We did not attempt to fill the vastness of the cathedral with all the garden produce dear to a parish church, but the dean was fond of fat sheaves of wheat, oats and barley, bound round the middle like sheaves on a heraldic shield.

It was his own festival in his own cathedral, so that he, not the bishop, conducted it. He had made the ritual as enjoyable as that of Christmas, reviving ancient customs for which he was always ready to quote authority. I suspect that medieval deans would have denied his interpretation of their scanty records, but they would have recognised a master of stage management.

His most effective revival was a procession of cathedral tenants and benefactors, each bearing some offering in kind which the dean received on the altar steps. Fruit, honey and cakes were common, always with some touch of magnificence in the quality, quantity or container. On one occasion, the landlord of the Pilgrim's Inn presented a roasted peacock set in jelly with tail feathers erect. There was some argument about this on the grounds that it ran close to advertisement. But the dean would not be dissuaded. He insisted that any craftsman had the right to present a unique specimen of his skill.

That year the gifts were more humble. My father, as always, led the procession with a basket tray upon which was a two-foot bunch of black grapes from the vinery in the canons' garden. A most original participant was a dear old nursery gardener who presented a plant of his new dwarf camellia which had been the botanical sensation of the year and could not yet be bought for money. There was also a noble milk-pan of Alpine strawberries and cream – which, we hoped, the cathedral school would share next day with the alms houses.

While the file of some twenty persons advanced into the chancel, the choir full-bloodedly sang the 65th Psalm to the joyous score of our own organist. The dean's sense of theatre was as faultless as ever. Lavish in ritual and his own vestments, he then played his part with the utmost simplicity. He thanked and blessed each giver almost conversationally.

Last in the procession were four boys of the cathedral school bearing a great silver bowl of nuts gathered in the hedgerows. The gift and their movements were traditional. As they separated, two to the right and two to the left, leaving the dean alone upon the altar steps, a shadow appeared at his feet and vanished so swiftly that by the time our eyes had registered its true, soft shape it was no longer there.

The dean bent down and picked up a dead field-mouse. He was not put out of countenance for a moment. He laid it reverently with the other gifts. No one was present to be thanked; but when the dean left the cathedral after service and stopped in the porch to talk to Abner he was – to the surprise of the general public – still wearing his full vestments, stiff, gorgeous and suggesting the power of the Church to protect and armour with its blessing the most humble of its servants.

Cat Cult

S. J. Forrest

Concerning a certain ascetic,
We have a quaint story to tell:
He gives up his bed to a puss-cat,
In terror of going to hell.

He preaches a vital religion,
For convent, or suburb, or flat,
Derived from the ancient Egyptians,
The worship and cult of a cat.

The essence of true veneration,
Without any flurry or fuss,
Consists in the manifestation
Of deference due to the puss.

The morning devotions are simple:
He kneels to his fetish of silk,
And pours out an ample libation,
The cream of the cream of the milk.

Though fasts, in the Church, are discarded,
He yields up his fish and his meat,
Conserving it all for his goddess,
Ensuring her plenty to eat.

The granular foods, from the packet,
He likens to venial sin;
And views it a sacrilege mortal,
To feed a fine cat from a TIN!

A daily routine is essential,
To sweep out her lair with a broom,
Remembering always, with homage,
To rise when she enters the room.

The task of preparing the cushions,
Requires dedication and care:
Let worshippers stand to attention
Until she has chosen her chair!

Away with the vile unbeliever,
Who gives the first place to the dog!
Conferring with scorn on the feline
The blasphemous title of 'Mog'.

Our Brother, secure in devotion,
Avers it is pleasing to find,
A faith with congenial purpose,
A goddess who knows her own mind.

The Trinity Cat

Ellis Peters

He was sitting on top of one of the rear gate-posts of the churchyard when I walked through on Christmas Eve, grooming in his lordly style, with one back leg wrapped round his neck, and his bitten ear at an angle of forty-five degrees, as usual. I reckon one of the toms he'd tangled with in his nomad days had ripped the starched bit out of that one; the other stood up sharply enough. There was snow on the ground, a thin veiling, just beginning to crackle in promise of frost before evening, but he had at least three warm refuges around the place whenever he felt like holing up, besides his two houses, which he used only for visiting and cadging. He'd been a known character around our village for three years then, ever since he walked in from nowhere and made himself agreeable to the vicar and the verger, and, finding the billet comfortable and the pickings good, constituted himself resident cat to Holy Trinity church, and took over all the jobs around the place that humans were too slow to tackle, like rat-catching, and chasing off invading dogs.

Nobody knows how old he is, but I think he could only have been about two when he settled here, a scrawny, chewed-up black bandit as lean as wire. After three years of being fed by Joel Woodward at Trinity Cottage, which was the verger's house by tradition, and flanked the lych-gate on one side, and pampered and petted by Miss Patience Thomson at Church Cottage on the other side, he was double his old size, and sleek as velvet, but still had one lop ear and a kink two inches from the end of his tail. He still looked like a brigand, but a highly prosperous brigand. Nobody ever gave him a name, he wasn't the sort to get called anything fluffy or familiar. Only Miss Patience ever dared coo at him, and he was very gracious about that, she being elderly and innocent and very free with little perks like raw liver, on which he doted. One way and another, he had it made. He lived mostly outdoors, never staying in either house overnight. In winter he had his own little ground-level hatch into the furnace-room of the church, sharing his lodgings matily with a hedgehog that had qualified as assistant vermin-destructor around the churchyard, and preferred sitting out the winter among the coke to hibernating like common hedgehogs. These individualists keep turning up in our valley, for some reason.

All I'd gone to the church for that afternoon was to fix up with the vicar about the Christmas peal, having been roped into the bell-ringing team. Resident police in remote areas like ours get dragged into all sorts of activities, and when the area's changing, and new problems cropping up, if they have any sense they don't need too much dragging, but go willingly. I've put my finger on many an astonished yobbo who thought he'd got clean away with his little breaking-and-entering, just by keeping my ears open during a darts match, or choir practice.

When I came back through the churchyard, around half-past two, Miss Patience was just coming out of her gate, with a shopping bag on her wrist, and heading towards the street, and we walked along together a bit of the way.

She was getting on for seventy, and hardly bigger than a bird, but very independent. Never having married or left the valley, and having looked after a mother who lived to be nearly ninety, she'd never had time to catch up with new ideas in the style of dress suitable for elderly ladies. Everything had always been done Mother's way, and fashion, music and morals had stuck at the period when mother was a carefully brought-up girl learning domestic skills, and preparing for a chaste marriage. There's a lot to be said for it! But it had turned Miss Patience into a frail little lady in long-skirted black or grey or navy blue, who still felt undressed without hat and gloves, at an age when Mrs Newcombe, for instance, up at the pub, favoured shocking pink trouser-suits and red-gold hairpieces. A pretty little old lady Miss Patience was, though, very straight and neat. It was a pleasure to watch her walk. Which is more than I could say for Mrs Newcombe in her trouser suit, especially from the back!

'A happy Christmas, Sergeant Moon!' she chirped at me on sight. And I wished her the same, and slowed up to her pace.

'It's going to be slippery by twilight,' I said. 'You be careful how you go.'

'Oh, I'm only going to be an hour or so,' she said serenely. 'I shall be home long before the frost sets in. I'm only doing the last bit of Christmas shopping. There's a cardigan I have to collect for Mrs Downs.' That was her cleaning-lady, who went in three mornings a week. 'I ordered it long ago, but deliveries are so slow nowadays. They've promised it for today. And a gramophone record for my little errand-boy.' Tommy Fowler, that was, one of the church trebles, as pink and wholesome-looking as they usually contrive to be, and just as artful. 'And one mustn't forget our dumb friends, either, must one?' said Miss Patience cheerfully. 'They're all important, too.'

I took this to mean a couple of packets of some new product to lure wild birds to her garden. The Church Cottage thrushes were so fat they could hardly fly, and when it was frosty she put out fresh water three or four times a day.

We came to our brief street of shops, and off she went, with her big jet-and-gold brooch gleaming in her scarf. She had quite a few pieces of Victorian and Edwardian jewellery her mother'd left behind, and almost always wore one piece, being used to the belief that a lady dresses meticulously every day, not just on Sundays. And I went for a brisk walk round to see what was going on, and then went home to Molly and high tea, and took my boots off thankfully.

That was Christmas Eve. Christmas Day little Miss Thomson didn't turn up for eight o'clock Communion, which was unheard-of. The vicar said he'd call in after matins and see that she was all right, and hadn't taken cold trotting about in the snow. But somebody else beat us both to it. Tommy Fowler! He was anxious about that pop record of his. But even he had no chance until after service, for in our village it's the custom for the choir to go and sing the vicar an aubade in the shape of 'Christians, Awake!' before the main service, ignoring the fact that he's then been up four hours, and conducted two Communions. And Tommy Fowler had a solo in the anthem, too. It was a quarter past twelve when he got away, and shot up the garden path to the door of Church Cottage.

He shot back even faster a minute later. I was heading for home when he came rocketing out of the gate and ran slam into me, with his eyes sticking out on stalks and his mouth wide open, making a sort of muted keening sound with

16

shock. He clutched hold of me and pointed back towards Miss Thomson's front door, left half-open when he fled, and tried three times before he could croak out:

'Miss Patience . . . She's there on the floor – she's bad!'

I went in on the run, thinking she'd had a heart attack all alone there, and was lying helpless. The front door led through a diminutive hall, and through another glazed door into the living-room, and that door was open, too, and there was Miss Patience face-down on the carpet, still in her coat and gloves, and with her shopping-bag lying beside her. An occasional table had been knocked over in her fall, spilling a vase and a book. Her hat was askew over one ear, and caved in like a trodden mushroom, and her neat grey bun of hair had come undone and trailed on her shoulder, and it was no longer grey but soiled brownish-black. She was dead and stiff. The room was so cold, you could tell those doors had been ajar all night.

The kid had followed me in, hanging on to my sleeve, his teeth chattering. 'I didn't open the door – it was open! I didn't touch her, or anything. I only came to see if she was all right, and get my record.'

It was there, lying unbroken, half out of the shopping-bag by her arm. She'd meant it for him, and I told him he should have it, but not yet, because it might be evidence, and we mustn't move anything. And I got him out of there quick, and gave him to the vicar to cope with, and went back to Miss Patience as soon as I'd telephoned for the outfit. Because we had a murder on our hands.

So that was the end of one gentle, harmless old woman, one of very many these days, battered to death because she walked in on an intruder who panicked. Walked in on him, I judged, not much more than an hour after I left her in the street. Everything about her looked the same as then,

17

the shopping-bag, the coat, the hat, the gloves. The only difference, that she was dead. No, one more thing! No handbag, unless it was under the body, and later, when we were able to move her, I wasn't surprised to see that it wasn't there. Handbags are where old ladies carry their money. The sneak-thief who panicked and lashed out at her had still had greed and presence of mind enough to grab the bag as he fled. Nobody'd have to describe that bag to me, I knew it well, soft black leather with an old-fashioned gilt clasp and a short handle, a small thing, not like the holdalls they carry nowadays.

She was lying facing the opposite door, also open, which led to the stairs. On the writing-desk by that door stood one of a pair of heavy brass candlesticks. Its fellow was on the floor beside Miss Thomson's body, and though the bun of hair and the felt hat had prevented any great spattering of blood, there was blood enough on the square base to label the weapon. Whoever had hit her had been just sneaking down the stairs, ready to leave. She'd come home barely five minutes too soon.

Upstairs, in her bedroom, her bits of jewellery hadn't taken much finding. She'd never thought of herself as having valuables, or of other people as coveting them. Her gold and turquoise and funereal jet and true-lover's-knots in gold and opals, and Mother's engagement and wedding rings, and her little Edwardian pendant watch set with seed pearls had simply lived in the small top drawer of her dressing-table. She belonged to an honest epoch, and it was gone, and now she was gone after it. She didn't even lock her door when she went shopping. There wouldn't have been so much as the warning of a key grating in the lock, just the door opening.

Ten years ago not a soul in this valley behaved differently from Miss Patience. Nobody locked doors, sometimes not even overnight. Some of us went on a fortnight's holiday and left the doors unlocked. Now we can't even put out the milk money until the milkman knocks at the door in person. If this generation likes to pride itself on its progress, let it! As for me, I thought suddenly that maybe the innocent was well out of it.

We did the usual things, photographed the body and the scene of the crime, the doctor examined her and authorised her removal, and confirmed what I'd supposed about the approximate time of her death. And the forensic boys lifted a lot of smudgy latents that weren't going to be of any use to anybody, because they weren't going to be on record, barring a million-to-one chance. The whole thing stank of the amateur. There wouldn't be any easy matching up of prints, even if they got beauties. One more thing we did for Miss Patience. We tolled the dead-bell for her on Christmas night, six heavy, muffled strokes. She was a virgin. Nobody had to vouch for it, we all knew. And let me point out, it is a title of honour, to be respected accordingly.

We'd hardly got the poor soul out of the house when the Trinity cat strolled in, taking advantage of the minute or two while the door was open. He got as far as the place on the carpet where she'd lain, and his fur and whiskers stood on end, and even his lop ear jerked up straight. He put his nose down to the pile of the Wilton, about where her shopping-bag and handbag must have lain, and started going round in interested circles, sniffing the floor and making little throaty noises that might have been distress, but sounded like pleasure. Excitement, anyhow. The chaps from the C. I. D. were still busy, and didn't want him under their feet, so I picked him up and took him with me when I went across to Trinity Cottage to talk to the verger. The cat never liked being picked up; after a minute he started clawing and cursing, and I put him down. He stalked away again at once, past the corner where people shot their dead flowers, out at the lych-gate, and straight back to sit on Miss Thomson's doorstep. Well, after all, he used to get fed there; he might well be uneasy at all these queer comings and goings. And they don't say 'as curious as a cat' for nothing, either.

I didn't need telling that Joel Woodward had had no hand in what had happened, he'd been nearest neighbour and good friend to Miss Patience for years, but he might have seen or heard something out of the ordinary. He was a little, wiry fellow, gnarled like a tree-root, the kind that goes on spry and active into his nineties, and then decides that's enough, and leaves overnight. His wife was dead long ago, and his daughter had come back to keep house for him after her husband deserted her, until she died, too, in a bus accident. There was just old Joel now, and the grandson she'd left with him, young Joel Barnett, nineteen, and a bit of a tearaway by his grandad's standards, but so far pretty innocuous by mine. He was a sulky, graceless sort, but he did work, and he stuck with the old man when many another would have lit out elsewhere.

'A bad business,' said old Joel, shaking his head. 'I only wish I could help you lay hands on whoever did it. But I only saw her yesterday morning about ten, when she took in the milk. I was round at the church hall all afternoon, getting things ready for the youth social they had last night; it was dark before I got back. I never saw or heard anything out of place. You can't see her living-room light from here, so there was no call to wonder. But the lad was here all afternoon. They only work till one, Christmas Eve. Then they all went boozing together for an hour or so, I expect, so I don't know exactly what time he got in, but he was here and had the tea on when I came home. Drop round in an hour or so and he should be here. He's gone round

20

to collect this girl he's mashing. There's a party somewhere tonight.'

I dropped round accordingly, and young Joel was there, sure enough, shoulder-length hair, frilled shirt, outsize lapels and all, got up to kill, all for the benefit of the girl his grandad had mentioned. And it turned out to be Connie Dymond, from the comparatively respectable branch of the family, along the canal-side. There were three sets of Dymond cousins, boys, no great harm in 'em but worth watching, but only this one girl in Connie's family. A good-looker, or at least most of the lads seemed to think so, she had a dozen or so on her string before she took up with young Joel. Big girl, too, with a lot of mauve eye-shadow and a mother-of-pearl mouth, in huge platform shoes and the fashionable drab granny-coat. But she was acting very prim and proper with old Joel around.

'Half past two when I got home,' said young Joel. 'Grandad was round at the hall, and I'd have gone round to help him, only I'd had a pint or two, and after I'd had me dinner I went to sleep, so it wasn't worth it by the time I woke up. Around four, that'd be. From then on I was here watching the telly, and I never saw nor heard a thing. But there was nobody else here, so I could be spinning you the yarn, if you want to look at it that way.'

He had a way of going looking for trouble before anybody else suggested it, there was nothing new about that. Still, there it was. One young fellow on the spot, and minus any alibi. There'd be plenty of others in the same case.

In the evening he'd been at the church social. Miss Patience wouldn't be expected there, it was mainly for the young, and anyhow, she very seldom went out in the evenings.

21

'*I* was there with Joel,' said Connie Dymond. 'He called for me at seven, I was with him all the evening. We went home to our place after the social finished, and he didn't leave till nearly midnight.'

Very firm about it she was, doing her best for him. She could hardly know that his movements in the evening didn't interest us, since Miss Patience had then been dead for some hours.

When I opened the door to leave, the Trinity cat walked in, stalking past me with a purposeful stride. He had a look round us all, and then made for the girl, reached up his front paws to her knees, and was on her lap before she could fend him off, though she didn't look as if she welcomed his attentions. Very civil he was, purring and rubbing himself against her coat sleeve, and poking his whiskery face into hers. Unusual for him to be effusive, but when he did decide on it, it was always with someone who couldn't stand cats. You'll have noticed it's a way they have.

'Shove him off,' said young Joel, seeing she didn't at all care for being singled out. 'He only does it to annoy people.'

And she did, but he only jumped on again, I noticed as I closed the door on them and left. It was a Dymond party they were going to, the senior lot, up at the filling station. Not much point in trying to check up on all her cousins and swains when they were gathered for a booze-up. Coming out of a hangover, tomorrow, they might be easy meat. Not that I had any special reason to look their way, they were an extrovert lot, more given to grievous bodily harm in street punch-ups than anything secretive. But it was wide open.

Well, we summed up. None of the lifted prints was on record, all we could do in that line was exclude all those that were Miss Thomson's. This kind of sordid little

22

opportunist break-in had come into local experience only fairly recently, and though it was no novelty now, it had never before led to a death. No motive but the impulse of greed, so no traces leading up to the act, and none leading away. Everyone connected with the church, and most of the village besides, knew about the bits of jewellery she had, but never before had anyone considered them as desirable loot. Victoriana now carry inflated values, and are in demand, but this still didn't look calculated, just wanton. A kid's crime, a teenager's crime. Or the crime of a permanent teenager. They start at twelve years old now, but there are also the shiftless louts who never get beyond twelve years old, even in their forties.

We checked all the obvious people, her part-time gardener – but he was demonstrably elsewhere at the time – and his drifter of a son, whose alibi was non-existent but voluble, the window-cleaner, a sidelong soul who played up his ailments and did rather well out of her, all the delivery men. Several there who were clear, one or two who could have been around, but had no particular reason to be. Then we went after all the youngsters who, on their records, were possibles. There were three with breaking-and-entering convictions, but if they'd been there they'd been gloved. Several others with petty theft against them were also without alibis. By the end of a pretty exhaustive survey the field was wide, and none of the runners seemed to be ahead of the rest, and we were still looking. None of the stolen property had so far showed up.

Not, that is, until the Saturday. I was coming from Church Cottage through the graveyard again, and as I came near the corner where the dead flowers were shot, I noticed a glaring black patch making an irregular hole in the veil of frozen snow that still covered the ground.

23

You couldn't miss it, it showed up like a black eye. And part of it was the soil and rotting leaves showing through, and part, the blackest part, was the Trinity cat, head down and back arched, digging industriously like a terrier after a rat. The bent end of his tail lashed steadily, while the remaining eight inches stood erect. If he knew I was standing watching him, he didn't care. Nothing was going to deflect him from what he was doing. And in a minute or two he heaved his prize clear, and clawed out to the light a little black leather handbag with a gilt clasp. No mistaking it, all stuck over as it was with dirt and rotting leaves. And he loved it, he was patting it and playing with it and rubbing his head against it, and purring like a steam-engine. He cursed, though, when I took it off him, and walked round and round me, pawing and swearing, telling me and the world he'd found it, and it was his.

It hadn't been there long. I'd been along that path often enough to know that the snow hadn't been disturbed the day before. Also, the mess of humus fell off it pretty quick and clean, and left it hardly stained at all. I held it in my handkerchief and snapped the catch, and the inside was clean and empty, the lining slightly frayed from long use. The Trinity cat stood upright on his hind legs and protested loudly, and he had a voice that could outshout a Siamese.

Somebody behind me said curiously: 'Whatever've you got there?' And there was young Joel standing open-mouthed, staring, with Connie Dymond hanging on to his arm and gaping at the cat's find in horrified recognition.

'Oh, no! My gawd, that's Miss Thomson's bag, isn't it? I've seen her carrying it hundreds of times.'

'Did *he* dig it up?' said Joel, incredulous. 'You reckon

the chap who – you know, *him!*—he buried it there? It could be anybody, everybody uses this way through.'

'My gawd!' said Connie, shrinking in fascinated horror against his side. 'Look at that cat! You'd think he *knows* . . . He gives me the shivers! What's got into him?'

What, indeed? After I'd got rid of them and taken the bag away with me I was still wondering. I walked away with his prize and he followed me as far as the road, howling and swearing, and once I put the bag down, open, to see what he'd do, and he pounced on it and started his fun and games again until I took it from him. For the life of me I couldn't see what there was about it to delight him, but he was in no doubt. I was beginning to feel right superstitious about this avenging detective cat, and to wonder what he was going to unearth next.

I know I ought to have delivered the bag to the forensic lab, but somehow I hung on to it overnight. There was something fermenting at the back of my mind that I couldn't yet grasp.

Next morning we had two more at morning service besides the regulars. Young Joel hardly ever went to church, and I doubt if anybody'd ever seen Connie Dymond there before, but there they both were, large as life and solemn as death, in a middle pew, the boy sulky and scowling as if he'd been press-ganged into it, as he certainly had, Connie very subdued and big-eyed, with almost no make-up and an unusually grave and thoughtful face. Sudden death brings people up against daunting possibilities, and creates penitents. Young Joel felt silly there, but he was daft about her, plainly enough, she could get him to do what she wanted, and she'd wanted to make this gesture. She went through all the movements of devotion, he just sat, stood and kneeled awkwardly as required, and went on scowling.

There was a bitter east wind when we came out. On the steps of the porch everybody dug out gloves and turned up collars against it, and so did young Joel, and as he hauled his gloves out of his coat pocket, out with them came a little bright thing that rolled down the steps in front of us all and came to rest in a crack between the flagstones of the path. A gleam of pale blue and gold. A dozen people must have recognised it. Mrs Downs gave tongue in a shriek that informed even those who hadn't.

'That's Miss Thomson's! It's one of her turquoise earrings! *How did you get hold of that, Joel Barnett?*'

How, indeed? Everybody stood staring at the tiny thing, and then at young Joel, and he was gazing at the flagstones, struck white and dumb. And all in a moment Connie Dymond had pulled her arm free of his and recoiled from him until her back was against the wall, and was edging away from him like somebody trying to get out of range of flood or fire, and her face a sight to be seen, blind and stiff with horror.

'You!' she said in a whisper. 'It was you! Oh, my God, *you* did it – *you* killed her! And me keeping company – how could I? How could *you?*'

She let out a screech and burst into sobs, and before anybody could stop her she turned and took to her heels, running for home like a mad thing.

I let her go. She'd keep. And I got young Joel and that single ear-ring away from the Sunday congregation and into Trinity Cottage before half the people there knew what was happening, and shut the world out, all but old Joel who came panting and shaking after us a few minutes later.

The boy was a long time getting his voice back, and when he did he had nothing to say but, hopelessly, over and over: 'I didn't! I never touched her, I wouldn't. I don't know how that thing got into my pocket. I didn't do it. I never . . .'

Human beings are not all that inventive. Given a similar set of circumstances they tend to come out with the same formula. And in any case, 'deny everything and say nothing else' is a very good rule when cornered.

They thought I'd gone round the bend when I said: 'Where's the cat? See if you can get him in.'

Old Joel was past wondering. He went out and rattled a saucer on the steps, and pretty soon the Trinity cat strolled in. Not at all excited, not wanting anything, fed and lazy, just curious enough to come and see why he was wanted. I turned him loose on young Joel's overcoat, and he couldn't have cared less. The pocket that had held the ear-ring held very little interest for him. He didn't care about any of the clothes in the wardrobe, or on the pegs in the little hall. As far as he was concerned, this new find was a non-event.

I sent for a constable and a car, and took young Joel in with me to the station, and all the village, you may be sure, either saw us pass or heard about it very shortly after. But I didn't stop to take any statement from him, just left him there, and took the car up to Mary Melton's place, where she breeds Siamese, and borrowed a cat-basket from her, the sort she uses to carry her queens to the vet. She asked what on earth I wanted it for, and I said to take the Trinity cat for a ride. She laughed her head off.

'Well, *he*'s no queen,' she said, 'and no king, either. Not even a jack! And you'll never get that wild thing into a basket.'

'Oh, yes, I will,' I said. 'And if he isn't any of the other picture cards, he's probably going to turn out to be the joker.'

A very neat basket it was, not too obviously meant for a cat. And it was no trick getting the Trinity cat into it, all

I did was drop in Miss Thomson's handbag, and he was in after it in a moment. He growled when he found himself shut in, but it was too late to complain then.

At the house by the canal Connie Dymond's mother let me in, but was none too happy about letting me see Connie, until I explained that I needed a statement from her before I could fit together young Joel's movements all through those Christmas days. Naturally I understood that the girl was terribly upset, but she'd had a lucky escape, and the sooner everything was cleared up, the better for her. And it wouldn't take long.

It didn't take long. Connie came down the stairs readily enough when her mother called her. She was all stained and pale and tearful, but had perked up somewhat with a sort of shivering pride in her own prominence. I've seen them like that before, getting the juice out of being the centre of attention even while they wish they were elsewhere. You could even say she hurried down, and she left the door of her bedroom open behind her, by the light coming through at the head of the stairs.

'Oh, Sergeant Moon!' she quavered at me from three steps up. 'Isn't it *awful*? I still can't believe it! *Can* there be some mistake? Is there any chance it *wasn't* . . . ?'

I said soothingly, yes, there was always a chance. And I slipped the latch of the cat-basket with one hand, so that the flap fell open, and the Trinity cat was out of there and up those stairs like a black flash, startling her so much she nearly fell down the last step, and steadied herself against the wall with a small shriek. And I blurted apologies for accidentally loosing him, and went up the stairs three at a time ahead of her, before she could recover her balance.

He was up on his hind legs in her dolly little room, full of pop posters and frills and garish colours, pawing at the second drawer of her dressing-table, and singing a loud, joyous, impatient song. When I came plunging in, he even looked over his shoulder at me and stood down, as though he knew I'd open the drawer for him. And I did, and he was up among her fancy undies like a shot, and digging with his front paws.

He found what he wanted just as she came in at the door. He yanked it out from among her bras and slips, and tossed it into the air, and in seconds he was on the floor with it, rolling and wrestling it, juggling it on his four paws like a circus turn, and purring fit to kill, a cat in ecstasy. A comic little thing it was, a muslin mouse with a plaited green nylon string for a tail, yellow beads for eyes, and nylon threads for whiskers, that rustled and sent out wafts of strong scent as he batted it around and sang to it. A catmint mouse, old Miss Thomson's last-minute purchase from the pet shop for her dumb friend. If you could ever call the Trinity cat dumb! The only thing she bought that day small enough to be slipped into her handbag instead of the shopping-bag.

Connie let out a screech, and was across that room so fast I only just beat her to the open drawer. They were all there, the little pendant watch, the locket, the brooches, the true-lover's-knot, the purse, even the other ear-ring. A mistake, she should have ditched both while she was about it, but she was too greedy. They were for pierced ears, anyhow, no good to Connie.

I held them out in the palm of my hand – such a large haul they made – and let her see what she'd robbed and killed for.

If she'd kept her head she might have made a fight of it even then, claimed he'd made her hide them for him, and she'd been afraid to tell on him directly, and could only think of staging that public act at church to get

29

him safely in custody before she came clean. But she went wild. She did the one deadly thing, turned and kicked out in a screaming fury at the Trinity cat. He was spinning like a humming-top, and all she touched was the kink in his tail. He whipped round and clawed a red streak down her leg through the nylon. And then she screamed again, and began to babble through hysterical sobs that she never meant to hurt the poor old sod, that it wasn't her fault! Ever since she'd been going with young Joel she'd been seeing that little old bag going in and out, draped with her bits of gold. What in hell did an old witch like her want with jewellery? She had no *right*! At her age!

'But I never meant to hurt her! She came in too soon,' lamented Connie, still and for ever the aggrieved. 'What was I supposed to do? I had to get away, didn't I? *She was between me and the door!*'

She was half her size, too, and nearly four times her age! Ah well! What the courts would do with Connie, thank God, was none of my business. I just took her in and charged her, and got her statement. Once we had her dabs it was all over, because she'd left a bunch of them sweaty and clear on that brass candlestick. But if it hadn't been for the Trinity cat and his single-minded pursuit, scaring her into that ill-judged attempt to hand us young Joel as a scapegoat, she might, she just might, have got clean away with it. At least the boy could go home now, and count his blessings.

Not that she was very bright, of course. Who but a stupid harpy, soaked in cheap perfume and gimcrack dreams, would have hung on even to the catmint mouse, mistaking it for a herbal sachet to put among her smalls?

I saw the Trinity cat only this morning, sitting grooming in the church porch. He's getting very self-important, as if he knows he's a celebrity, though throughout he was only looking after the interests of Number One, like all cats. He's lost interest in his mouse already, now most of the scent's gone.

The Presbyterian Cat

Anon.

There was a Presbyterian cat
Went forth to catch her prey;
She brought a mouse intill the house,
Upon the Sabbath Day.
The minister, offended
With such an act profane,
Laid down his book, the cat he took,
And bound her with a chain.

Thou vile, malicious creature,
Thou murderer, said he,
Oh, do you think to bring to Hell
My holy wife and me?
But be thou well assured,
That blood for blood shall pay,
For taking of the mouse's life
Upon the Sabbath Day.

Then he took doun his Bible,
And fervently he prayed
That the great sin the cat had done
Might not on him be laid.
Then forth to execution,
Poor Baudrons she was drawn,
And on a tree they hanged her hie,
And then they sung a psalm.

The Devout Cat

I. L. Peretz

Once upon a time there were three little singing birds in a house, but all three were devoured by the cat. It was not an ordinary cat, but a really, really devout cat. It was not in vain that it was arrayed in a white robe of immaculate purity, and that its eyes reflected the heavens.

It was a pious cat, a cat that scrupulously performed all its ablutions. Ten times a day would this cat wash itself; and as for food, it devoured it very quietly, lying curled up in an obscure corner. It fed all the day on a modest milk diet and only in the evening did it partake of a bit of meat, the kosher meat of some mouse. And then again this cat, unlike those of a grosser nature, did not hurry over its food, or gorge itself like a glutton, but ate slowly, whilst playing with its victim. 'Why not let the little mouse live another few minutes?' thought the devout cat. 'Let the poor mite dance a little while, tremble, and make its confession; a really pious cat never hurries.'

When the first singing bird was brought into the house, the cat at once felt great pity for the bird and its heart grew constricted.

'Such a beautiful, tiny thing,' sighed the compassionate cat, 'and to think that such a nice little bird will never enjoy celestial bliss.' For, of course, the cat was fully convinced that a little bird like that could not deserve heaven. 'First of all a bird washes itself in a vulgar way, plunging its whole body into a basin of water. Then, again, the very fact that it is put in a cage proves it to be a very wicked animal. In spite of its still being very young, gentle, and kind, this bird is already showing an inclination towards violence rather than law and order. And what about its song? Its song, to say the least, is full of effrontery, and its manner of looking straight up to heaven is quite disrespectful. And think of all its efforts to break the cage and fly out into the impious world, into the free air; think also of its look turned to the open window. Have you ever seen a cat shut up in a cage? Has a pious cat ever ventured to whistle with such effrontery? The pity of it,' sighed the tender-hearted and devout cat, 'for, after all, it is a living being, possessed of a precious soul, a spark from above.'

Tears welled up in the eyes of the pious and devout cat.

'All its misfortune is due to the fact of its possessing such a beautiful sinful body, a body attracted to terrestrial pleasures and joys, over which the spirit of temptation has so much sway. How can you expect such a gentle little bird to be able to resist the terrible spirit of temptation? And the longer the poor thing lives,' thought the devout cat, 'the greater the number of sins it will commit, and the more terrible its punishment in the hereafter.'

A sacred fire enflamed the heart of the devout cat. Jumping upon the table where stood the cage with the little bird, it . . . The feathers were soon scattered over the room.

Blows rained upon the cat, but it accepted its punishment with humility, as behoves a devout cat. Sighing piously, it began to mew, to groan in pious resignation, reciting a pitiable *mea culpa*. In future the cat will not commit such an error, for being a reasonable cat, it understood why it had been beaten. Henceforth it will never deserve such blows.

'I have been beaten,' reasoned the devout cat, 'because I have scattered the feathers all over the room, and also because I have left traces of blood all over the white and embroidered tablecloth. When executing such sentences, one ought to proceed with kindness, with gentleness, and piety; one must never scatter the feathers nor spill a drop of blood.'

When the second bird was bought and brought into the house, the pious cat acted quite differently. This time it strangled the little bird gently and delicately, and swallowed it whole, body and feathers. Nevertheless the cat was soundly thrashed.

This time the cat understood that it was not at all a question of either feathers or traces of blood left on the tablecloth. The secret of its punishment lay in the fact that it was a sin to kill. On the contrary, one must love and forgive. It is not by means of punishments and tortures that we can reform and save a world steeped in sin. What is required of us is to lead the sinful creatures upon the path of virtue, preach morals to them, and appeal to their hearts.

A repentant canary can soar to lofty summits in heaven, unattainable even for a devout cat. And the heart of the cat swelled with joy. Over were the old, hard, cruel, and wicked days. Over was the shedding of blood. Pity was the watchword, pity, and once more pity. And it was a cat full of pity that approached the third canary.

'Don't be afraid,' said the cat in the most gentle voice that ever issued from a cat's throat. 'It is true thou art steeped in sin, but I will do thee no harm, for my heart is full of pity for thee.

'I will not even open thy cage, I will even refrain from touching thee.

'Thou art silent? Excellent. It is better to be silent than to sing impudently.

'Thou art trembling? It is better still. Tremble, my child, but not on account of me!

'May it please God that thou shouldst remain thus gently pure and trembling.

'As for me, I will help thee to tremble. From the depth of my pious soul I will breathe upon thee the spirit of calmness, of gentleness and piety. May my pious breath instil into thy body profound faith, may divine fear penetrate into thy little bones, and may remorse and repentance fill thy little heart.'

It was now only that the devout cat understood how sweet forgiveness was, what holy joy one may derive from the action of breathing into others the spirit of piety and of virtue. And the heart of the most pious and devout of white cats swelled for joy and happiness. But, alas, the canary could not breathe in the atmosphere of the cat. It was stifled.

Pangur Bán *

Anon.

translated from the Gaelic by Robin Flower

I and Pangur Bán, my cat,
'Tis a like task we are at;
Hunting mice is his delight,
Hunting words I sit all night.

Better far than praise of men
'Tis to sit with book and pen;
Pangur bears me no ill-will,
He too plies his simple skill.

'Tis a merry thing to see
At our tasks how glad are we,
When at home we sit and find
Entertainment to our mind.

* This poem about a scholar and his cat was written in Gaelic on
a copy of St Paul's Epistles by a ninth-century Irish monk at the
monastery of Carinthia in Reichnau on the shores of Lake Constance,
Switzerland. *Pangur* means white in Gaelic, so presumably the cat
was white.

Oftentimes a mouse will stray
In the hero Pangur's way;
Oftentimes my keen thought set
Takes a meaning in its net.

'Gainst the wall he sets his eye
Full and fierce and sharp and sly;
'Gainst the wall of knowledge I
All my little wisdom try.

When a mouse darts from its den,
O how glad is Pangur then!
O what gladness do I prove
When I solve the doubts I love!

So in peace our tasks we ply,
Pangur Bán, my cat, and I;
In our arts we find our bliss,
I have mine and he has his.

Practice every day has made
Pangur perfect in his trade;
I get wisdom day and night
Turning darkness into light.

The Cure

George Mackay Brown

Not two hundred yards from Jenny's father's croft stood the island church, and beside it the manse where the minister lived with his elderly mother Mrs Martin. It was a sad house, because poor Mrs Martin had not been at all well for years. What was wrong with her nobody knew, not even the island doctor. It was just that the kind old lady was melancholy all the time now. Her sad eyes looked out at a sad world. She didn't see the point of going out any longer, when there was nothing but sadness and vanity to be seen and heard. If she went anywhere, she reasoned, she would only intensify the existing sadness. Indoors there was little solace for her either, though her son Andrew was all considerateness and kindness. Her food tasted of nothing. The books she had loved once bored her now. Sometimes she would take up wool and knitting needles, but all she knitted was an immensely long, grey, scarf-like garment that grew and grew and was now fifteen feet long if it was an inch.

'Mother,' said the Rev. Andrew Martin one morning after breakfast (which he had prepared and set, for she wasn't interested in cooking either), 'Mother, it's such a beautiful day! There are only two little clouds like white

41

lambs in the sky. Everything is so beautiful and warm and clear. It's a shame to be indoors. You really must sit outside on a morning like this. I'll bring your chair and your shawl.'

'If you like,' said Mrs Martin dully. And she was sorry her words were so leaden and dispirited, for she didn't like hurting her son; and because she loved him, and because the morning through the sitting-room window was so radiant, her spirits sank lower than ever.

Andrew wrestled the huge fireside chair outside and set it just beside the door, and he arranged the cushion. Mrs Martin came out like Mary Queen of Scots approaching the scaffold. She sighed and sat down. Andrew draped the shawl about her shoulders.

'Bring my knitting,' she said.

Having seen her as comfortable as possible, Andrew retired to his study to work on his Sunday sermon, and the old lady was alone.

And really, it was such a beautiful morning! A blackbird sang from the garden wall, burst after burst of purest ecstasy! The two little clouds like lambs had been joined by a third, high up in the intense blue sky, but they seemed to be too tranced with delight to move. The sea, between the two green hills, shimmered. You could almost feel the joy of the grass growing, and the teeming wildflowers. You could, if you were not Mrs Martin. She sat there, the sole blight on this happy summer world. As she sat, a tear welled in her eye – melancholy's answer to the dewdrop in the heart of the garden rose.

She took up her knitting needles, but they made an ugly 'clack-clack' in the delicate web of sound that lay over the island. She dropped them again.

Just then, Mrs Martin saw a black cat on the garden wall, magnified and distorted by the unfallen tears in her eyes.

Of course, it was the cat of Inquoy, Jan Thomson's croft. What was its name now – Flannel? Funnel? Mrs Martin couldn't quite remember. Some funny name like that. And it was a strange cat too. It followed the Thomson girl to school most mornings. It had (so she'd heard) attacked the coastguard's Alsatian dog – flown in his face like a black whirlwind, claws and teeth out – and sent the huge powerful dog home with his tail between his legs. And here it was now, on the garden wall of the manse. That had never happened before.

The cat seemed to be taking a friendly interest in the creature he shared the wall with – the joyous blackbird. The blackbird was too busy keeping a wary eye on the cat to sing now. It quivered on the wall, poised for flight, should that sinister shadow make one move.

Really, thought Mrs Martin, if there is to be any 'nature red in tooth and claw' in this garden, I'll call Andrew to take me inside. I just *couldn't* stand that!

And then she realised that the black cat was looking at her, in a very concerned way. He looked, and looked, and then leapt softly from the wall on to the lawn, and approached her.

The blackbird resumed its song, a magnificent fount of celebration.

You would almost think the cat had some kind of message for Mrs Martin. But in the long garden there were so many distractions. First it was the butterflies. Three of them exploded silently out of the rosebush over Fankle's face. He fought with them for several seconds, but butterflies are much harder to fight against than dogs, and the butterflies separated, drifting airily each his own way. Fankle didn't seem to mind such a lyrical defeat. Once more he turned a serious regard on poor afflicted Mrs Martin.

What now – whatever was the creature doing now? He seemed to have found something in the long grass. Delicately he howked it out with a fore-paw, and it was – a fragment of cherry-cake! Mrs Martin was *astonished*. The duplicity of Andrew! So this was what he did in the garden, late in the evening, after she was in bed – eat cherry-cake – slice after slice of it, she wouldn't wonder. The thing was, Andrew had become worried last winter that he was 'digging his grave with his teeth'. It was sweet things that he had always gone for, from his childhood up – chocolate, cream buns, meringues, honey and bread, but chiefly and most of all: *cherry-cake*. Cherry-cake was the chief villain in the thrilling drama that was going on in Andrew's body. Cherry-cake he loved passionately and devotedly – and it was cherry-cake that would finish Andrew off. So Andrew believed. It was true, he seemed to be getting fatter with every month that passed, and he was deeply worried about it. Last winter Andrew had come to a solemn decision – no more sweet things for him. He renounced them, he put them behind him. He got a diet sheet from the doctor which he studied carefully. Above all, cherry-cake, which had been his joy and delight, was to be banned for ever from the manse.

Be sure your sins will find you out! So this was what Andrew did night after night, in the garden, when he was supposed to be studying the growth of potatoes and lettuce and strawberries – he was wolfing down, in secret, thick slices of cherry-cake!

Mrs Martin didn't know whether to laugh or cry. If it had been a really serious business – if Andrew was indeed cherry-caking himself to death – there would have been cause for tears. But the truth was, Andrew was and had always been an acute hypochondriac, forever worried about his health. The island doctor had assured

Mrs Martin, privately, that there was nothing wrong with Andrew – he could eat, with safety, as much cherry-cake as he wanted. And Mrs Martin had told the doctor in return that stoutness ran in the family: Andrew's father and uncle and grandfather had been even huger than Andrew – vast men who set the earth trembling under their feet.

It had taken this cat to discover Andrew's innocent deceit. A fair fragment of cherry-cake Andrew must have dropped and not found in the twilight of last night! The black cat swallowed the cherry, his eyes melting with sheer sensuous delight.

'You *are* a strange cat,' said Mrs Martin out loud. The blackbird agreed with her, thrillingly. Fankle himself seemed to acquiesce. He approached the invalid obliquely, across the shallot bed.

Then, before Mrs Martin was aware of it, he pounced! He pushed the ball of grey wool away, he parried, dancingly he threatened it – you would think he both loved and hated it. Then something happened: his claw got hooked in the endless scarf that Mrs Martin was knitting, and he could not get the paw free. He tugged, he pulled. The knitting needles fell with a tiny clatter on the flagstones. Fankle whirled about, and that was the worst thing he could have done, for the scarf began to drape itself about him, and the harder the cat tugged and struggled, the closer he was wound. The struggle to escape went on for the duration of two blackbird songs, and at the end of it Fankle lay there on the grass at Mrs Martin's feet like a badly put-together Egyptian mummy. Even his head was covered – one ear only stuck out. At last, from inside the grey swathe, emerged a tiny 'miaow'.

'Andrew,' cried Mrs Martin.

Her stout son was there in five seconds, his pen in his hand.

'Free that cat, Andrew,' said Mrs Martin.

'Good gracious!' said Andrew. 'How on earth did this happen?' And then, when he had unwound Fankle and unhooked the claw, 'Why, it's the Thomsons' cat – Fankle.'

'Fankle, is that its name?' said Mrs Martin. 'Well, Andrew, since you've been so good as to free Fankle, you can have a thick slice of cherry-cake.'

At the gape of guilty astonishment Andrew gave, she began to laugh: first a slow smile, then a reluctant chuckle, then a full-throated shout of merriment. It was just like the happy Mrs Martin of seven years ago, before the melancholy had come on her. It was, to Andrew, the most beautiful sound in all that summer of music and poetry.

As for Fankle, he gathered himself together with dignity, and left the garden without another glance at Mrs Martin and the Rev. Andrew Martin. He even ignored the blackbird.

It would be wrong to say that Mrs Martin was entirely cured of her depressions from that day on. She still sighed occasionally, and thought with sadness of the emptiness of existence and the pain of life. But she could go out – a thing that had never happened for seven years. She could visit the crofts, and speak to the old women and the children. She could shop at the village store. She sat once more in her pew in the kirk on Sundays. The whole island was the better of that, because they had always liked Mrs Martin.

Every Friday afternoon a little box was delivered at the door of Inquoy croft, addressed in Mrs Martin's writing to *FANKLE THOMSON*. Inside was a tin of salmon, Fankle's favourite food. At tea-time on Fridays, Fankle ate with great luxury.

The Rev. Andrew Martin resumed his eating of cherry-cake publicly, and grew rather fatter, but it suited him; and now he didn't mind so much, when there was laughter once more across the breakfast table at the manse.

Black Cat in Church

Eleanor Glenn Wallis

Prowling on silken paws
   Beneath the chancel rail,
He numbers those who kneel in prayer
   And swings a thoughtful tail.
Crouching as sooty and sleek as sin
   Before the altar stone,
He turns his tail upon the light
   And looks the devil's own.
Fearing the parson, close at hand,
   Will sternly exorcise him,
He plans to gather certain souls
   Before his Reverence spies him.

The Cat and the Cornfield

Bryan MacMahon

In Ireland, all you need to make a story is two men with completed characters – say, a parish priest and his sexton. There at once you have conflict. When, as a foil for the sexton, you throw in a mature tinker girl, wild and lissom, love interest is added to conflict. And when, finally, you supply a snow-white cat, a cornfield, and a shrewish woman who asks three questions, the parts, if properly put together, should at least provide a moderate tale.

The scene is laid in a village asleep on a summer hill: the hour of the day is mid-morning. The village is made up of a church that lacks a steeple, a pair of pubs – one thatched and the other slated – with maybe a dozen higgledy-piggledy houses divided equally as between thatch and slate. The gaps between the houses yield glimpses of well-foliaged trees beyond which the countryside falls away into loamy fields.

On the morning of our story, the sexton, a small grumpy fellow of middle age with irregular red features, by name Denny Furey, had just finished sweeping out the brown flagstones of the church porch. He then took up the wire mat at the door and tried irritably but vainly to shake three pebbles out of it.

At the sound of the rattling pebbles, the sexton's white cat which was sitting on the sunny wall of the church beside his master's cabin, looked up and mewed soundlessly.

Denny glanced sourly at the cat. 'Pangur Bán,' he said, 'if you didn't sleep in my breeches and so have 'em warm before my shanks on frosty mornings, I'd have you drowned long 'go!' The cat – he had pale green eyes and a blotch on his nose – silently mewed his misunderstanding.

Suddenly there came a sound of harness bells. A tinker's spring-cart, painted bright green and blue, with a shaggy piebald cob between the shafts, drew slowly past the church gate. Sitting on the near wing of the cart was a tinker girl wearing a tartan dress and a bright shoulder-shawl. Eighteen, perhaps; more likely, nineteen. She had wild fair hair and a nut-brown complexion. Spying the sexton struggling with the mat, her eyes gleamed with puckish pleasure.

Meeting her gaze, Denny grimaced ill-temperedly and then half-turned his back on her. As on a thought he swung around to scowl her a reminder of her duty. Slowly the girl cut the sign of the Cross on herself.

Just beyond the church gateway, the cob's lazy motion came to a halt. The girl continued to stare at the sexton. Angrily Denny dropped the mat. Swiftly he raised his right hand as if he had been taken with a desire to shout: 'Shoo! Be off with yourself at once!' The words refused to come.

Pangur Bán raised himself on shuddering legs, arched his back and sent a gracious but soundless mew of welcome in the girl's direction.

'That you may be lucky, master!' the tinker girl said. Then: 'Your wife – have she e'er an old pair of shoes?'

'Wife! Wife! I've no wife!' Denny turned sharply away and snatched up his brush.

The girl watched as the sexton's movements of sweeping became indefinably jaunty. Then her smiling eyes roved and rested for a moment on the thatched cabin at the left of the church gate.

Without turning round, Denny shouted: 'Nothing for you today!'

The girl was slow in replying. Her eyes still fast on the cabin, she said: 'I know you've nothin' for me, master!' She did not draw upon the reins.

Denny stopped brushing. His stance indicated that again he was struggling to say: 'Be off!' Instead of speaking, he set his brush against the church wall, turned his head without moving his shoulders and looked fully at the girl. She answered his eyes with frankness. They kept looking at one another for a long time. At last, his altering gaze still locked in hers, Denny turned his body around.

As if caught in drowse Denny donned his hat, then walked slowly towards the church gate. Lost rosaries clinked as the white-painted iron yielded to his fingers. Denny looked to left and to right. Up to this their eyes had been bound fast to one another.

The sunlit village was asleep. Pangur Bán lay curled and still on the warm wall.

A strange tenderness glossed Denny's voice. 'Where are you headin' for?' he asked. The gate latched shut behind him.

'Wherever the cob carries me!'

Again the girl's gaze swivelled to the cabin. 'Is that your house?' she asked, and then, as she glanced again at the wall: 'Is that your cat?'

'Ay! . . . Ay!'

For a long while the girl kept looking at the little house with its small deeply recessed windows. She noted well

53

the dark-green half-door above which shone a latch of polished brass.

'Do you never tire of the road?' Denny asked.

'Do you never tire of being fettered?' the girl flashed. She had turned to look at him directly.

Both sighed fully and deeply. Under the black hat Denny's eyes had begun to smoulder.

Secretly the girl dragged on the rein. As the cob shifted from one leg to another, she uttered a small exclamation of annoyance. Her red and green skirt made a wheel as she leaped from the vehicle and advanced to make an obscure adjustment to the harness. This done she prepared to lead her animal away.

Denny glanced desperately around. Uproad stood a hissing gander with his flock of geese serried behind him.

'I'll convey you apass the gander!' he blurted.

The tinker girl glanced at the gander; her mouth-corners twitched in a smile. She made a great to-do about gathering up the reins and adjusting her shawl. As she led the animal away, Denny moved to the far side of the road and kept pace with her as she went. Walking thus, apart yet together, they left the village and stepped downhill. Once the sexton glanced fearfully over his shoulder; the village was not so much asleep as stone-dead.

As the white road twisted, the village on the hillock was unseen. The cob – a hairy, bony animal – moved swiftly on the declivity so that Denny had to hurry to keep up with the girl and her animal.

The splendour of the summer accompanied them. The gauds of the harness were winking in the bright light. The countryside was a silver shield inclining to gold. Their footfalls were muted in the limestone road dust. Muted also were the noise of the horse's unshod hooves and the ringing of the harness bells. At last they came to the foot of the hillock. Here the road ran between level fields. Denny looked over his shoulder and saw Pangur Bán fifty yards behind him walking stealthily on the road margin.

'Be off!' the sexton shouted.

Pangur Bán paused to utter his soundless mew.

The girl smiled. They walked on for a space. Again Denny turned. 'Be off, you Judas!' he shouted. He snatched up a stone and flung it at the cat.

The instant the stone left the sexton's hand, Pangur judged that it was going to miss him. He remained utterly without movement. When the stone had gone singing away into stillness, the cat went over and smelled at a piece of road metal the bounding stone had disturbed. Pangur mewed his mystification into the sky; then spurted faithfully on.

The road again twisted. Now it was commanded by the entrance to the village on the hillock.

Here in a cornfield at the left-hand side of the road, the ripening corn was on the swing from green to gold. The field was a house of brightness open to the southern sky. Directly beside their boots a gap offered descent to the sown ground. The cob stopped dead and began to crop the roadside grass.

'Let us sit in the sun,' the sexton ventured. He indicated the remote corner of the cornfield.

The girl smiled in dreamy agreement. With slow movements she tied her cob to the butt of a whitethorn bush. The pair walked along by the edge of the corn and sat down on the grassy edge of the farthest headland. Here the corn screened them from the view of a person passing on the road. The fierceness and lushness of growth in this sun-trap had made the hedge behind them impenetrable. Denny set his hat back on his poll. Then he took the girl's hand in his and began to fondle it. Points of sweat appeared on his agitated face.

Twice already, from the top of the grassy fence, Pangur Bán had stretched out a paw in an attempt to descend into the cornfield. On each occasion thistles and thorns tipping his pads had dissuaded him from leaping. Through slim upended ovals of dark pupil the cat ruefully eyed the cropping horse, then turned to mew his upbraidings in the direction of his master. Tiring of this, he settled himself patiently to wait.

Pangur Bán sat with his tail curled around his front paws. His eyes were reluctant to open in the sunlight. His ears began to sift the natural sounds of the day.

Reading his Office, the huge old priest walked the village. Glancing up from his breviary, he noticed the brush idle against the church wall: he also spied the wire mat that lay almost concealed on the lawn grass. The impudence of the gander the priest punished with a wave of his blackthorn stick. Standing on the road in front of the sexton's cabin, he sang out: 'Denny! Denny Furey!' There was no reply.

The priest shuffled to the church door and in a lowered voice again called for his sexton. At last, with an angry shrug of his shoulders, he again turned his attention to his breviary. Still reading, he sauntered downhill and out into the open country.

After a while he raised his eyes. First he saw the brown-and-white pony, then he spied the flame that was the cat burning white beside the olive cornfield.

The old man's face crinkled. He grunted. Imprisoning his stick in his left armpit, he began to slouch in the direction of Pangur Bán. From time to time his eyes strayed over the gilt edging and the coloured markers of his book.

Denny glanced up from his sober love-making.

'Divine God!' he exclaimed.

The girl was leaning back on the grass: her doing so had tautened a swath of green hay to silver. She was smiling up at the sky as she spaced her clean teeth along a grass stem.

Reaching the cat, the priest halted. 'Pangur Bán,' he wheedled in a low voice. His eyes were roving over the cornfield. The cat tilted his back against the lower may leaves, set his four paws together and drooped as if for a bout of languid gaiety.

For a moment or two the priest tricked with the cat. Then he threw back his shoulders. 'To think that I don't see you, Denny Furey!' he clarioned.

Denny and the girl were silent and without movement. About them the minute living world asserted itself in the snip of grasshoppers.

Again the priest thundered: 'Nice example for a sexton!'

The sweat beaded above Denny's eyebrows. His thighs began to shiver in the breeches his cat slept in. The girl peered at the priest through the altering lattice of the corn-heads. Her expression was quizzical as she glanced at Denny.

From the roadway came again the dreaded voice: 'If it's the last thing I do, Denny Furey, I'll strip you of your black coat!'

At this moment a shrewish woman, wearing a black and green shawl, thrust around the bend of the road. She was resolutely headed for the village.

Seeing the woman approach, the priest quickly turned his face away from the cornfield and resumed his pacing along the road. His lips grew busy with the Latin psalms.

Peeping out and recognising the newcomer, Denny

Furey at first swore softly, then he began to moan. 'The parish will be ringin' with the news before dark!' he sniffled.

The woman blessed the priest so as to break him from his Office, then in a tone of voice that expressed thin concern: 'Did I hear your voice raised, Father?'

The priest lowered his shaggy eyebrows. 'Sermons don't sprout on bushes, my good woman!'

'Ah! Practisin' you were!'

Her crafty eyes alighted on the white cat. 'Would it be bird-chasin' the sexton's cat is?'

'It could be, now that you mention it!'

There was a pause. The conversation of the wheat spars was only one step above silence. Flicking the cornfield and the cart with a single glance, the woman said, in a half whisper: 'People say that tinker girls'd pick the eye out of your head!'

'Did you never hear tell of the virtue of charity, woman?' the priest growled.

The woman made her grumbled excuses. It suited the priest not to accept them. Hurriedly she walked away. Resentment was implicit in the puffs of road-dust that spouted from beneath her toe-caps. Before the village swallowed her up, she looked over her shoulder. The priest was standing in mid-road waiting to parry this backward glance.

Again the priest turned his attention to the cornfield. With a sound half-grunt, half-chuckle, he untied the cob, and leading it by the head, turned away in the direction of the village.

The instant the harness bells began to ring, the tinker girl sprang to her feet and raced wildly but surefootedly along the edge of the cornfield. 'Father!' she cried out. 'Father!'

The priest came to a halt. Well out of the range of his stick, the girl stopped. 'So I've drawn you, my vixen!' the priest said.

Breathlessly, the girl bobbed a half-curtsey.

'What're you goin' to do with my animal, Father?'

'Impounding him I am – unless you get that sexton o' mine out of the cornfield at once.'

The girl leaped on to the low fence: 'Come out o' the cornfield,' she shouted, 'I want to recover my cob!'

There was a pause. Then Denny shuffled to his feet. The cat stood up and mewed loyal greetings to his lord.

The priest stood at the horse's head. The angry girl was on the fence, her arms akimbo. Shambling dismally, Denny drew nearer. When he had reached the roadway, the tinker girl cried out: 'I was goin' my road, Father, when he coaxed me into the cornfield!'

Denny opened his mouth, but no words came. He began to blink his moist eyes. His mouth closed fast. He kept his distance from the priest's stick. As Pangur Bán began rubbing himself against the end of the beloved breeches, the sexton gave the cat the side of his long boot and sent him careering into the bushes.

'*A chait*, ou'r that!' he said.

'Aha, you scoundrel!' the priest reproved, 'Can you do no better than abuse a dumb animal?'

Turning to the girl: 'Take your cob! And if I catch you in this village again, by the Holy Man, I'll give you the length and breadth of my blackhorn!'

'He said he'd convey me apass the gander, Father!'

Three times she lunged forward. Three times her buttocks winced away. At last she mustered courage enough to grasp the winkers. Clutching the ring of the mouthpiece, she swung the pony downroad. When she had gained a few yards she leaped lightly on to the broad board on the side of the cart and slashed at the cob's rump with the free dangle of the reins. The animal leaped forward.

The priest, the sexton, the cat. The sunlit, rustling cornfield.

'Come on, me bucko!' the priest said grimly.

He began to lead the way home. The sexton trailed a miserable yard or two behind. Glory was gone out of his life. The wonderful day seemed to mock him. The future was a known road stretching before his leaden legs. What he had thought would prove a pleasant bauble had turned to a crown of thorns. In the past, whenever he had chafed against the drab nature of his existence, he had consoled himself thus: 'One day, perhaps today, I'll run and buy me a hoop of bright colours.'

Denny began to compare his soul to a pebble trapped in a wire mat of despair.

Gradually the priest became infected with Denny's moroseness. Side by side, the priest and his sexton continued to move homewards. In the faraway, the sound of the harness bells was a recessional song of adventure.

Behind the pair and at a discreet distance, Pangur Bán travelled quietly. Now and again he paused to mew his loyalty into the sunny world.

Of Jeoffry, His Cat *

Christopher Smart

For I will consider my Cat Jeoffry.

For he is the servant of the Living God, duly and daily
serving him.

For at the first glance of the glory of God in the East he
worships in his way.

For is this done by wreathing his body seven times
round with elegant quickness.

For then he leaps up to catch the musk, wch is the
blessing of God upon his prayer.

For he rolls upon prank to work it in.

For having done duty and received blessing he begins to
consider himself.

For this he performs in ten degrees.

For first he looks upon his fore-paws to see if they
are clean.

For secondly he kicks up behind to clear away there.

* The poet Christopher Smart (1722–71) suffered in later life from
intense religious mania which took the form of a compulsion to
public prayer, regarding which Dr Johnson famously declared, 'I'd
as lief pray with Kit Smart as anyone else.' These verses are taken
from *Jubilate Agno* (Rejoice in the Lamb).

For thirdly he works it upon stretch with the fore-paws
  extended.

For fourthly he sharpens his paws by wood.

For fiftly [sic] he washes himself.

For sixthly he rolls upon wash.

For Seventhly he fleas himself, that he may not be
  interrupted upon the beat.

For Eightly [sic] he rubs himself against a post.

For Ninthly he looks up for his instructions.

For Tenthly he goes in quest of food.

For having consider'd God and himself he will consider
  his neighbour.

For if he meets another cat he will kiss her in kindness.

For when he takes his prey he plays with it to give
  it chance.

For one mouse in seven escapes by his dallying.

For when his day's work is done his business more
  properly begins.

For [he] keeps the Lord's watch in the night against the
  adversary.

For he counteracts the powers of darkness by his
  electrical skin & glaring eyes.

For he counteracts the Devil, who is death, by brisking
  about the life.

For in his morning orisons he loves the sun and the sun
  loves him.

For he is of the tribe of Tiger.

For the Cherub Cat is a term of the Angel Tiger.

For he has the subtlety and hissing of a serpent, which in
  goodness he suppresses.

For he will not do destruction, if he is well fed, neither
  will he spit without provocation.

For he purrs in thankfulness, when God tells him he's a
  good Cat.

For he is an instrument for the children to learn
benevolence upon.

For every house is incompleat without him & a blessing
is lacking in the spirit.

For the Lord commanded Moses concerning the cats at
the departure of the Children of Israel from Egypt.

For every family had one cat at least in the bag.

For the English Cats are the best in Europe.

For he is the cleanest in the use of his fore-paws of any
quadrupede.

For the dexterity of his defence is an instance of the love
of God to him exceedingly.

For he is the quickest to his mark of any creature.

For he is tenacious of his point.

For he is a mixture of gravity and waggery.

For he knows that God is his Saviour.

For there is nothing sweeter than his peace when at
rest.

For there is nothing brisker than his life when in
motion.

For he is of the Lord's poor and so indeed is he called by
benevolence perpetually – Poor Jeoffry! poor Jeoffry!
the rat has bit thy throat.

For I bless the name of the Lord Jesus that Jeoffry
is better.

For the divine spirit comes about his body to sustain it in
compleat cat.

For his tongue is exceeding pure so that it has in purity
what it wants in musick.

For he is docile and can learn certain things.

For he can set up with gravity, which is patience upon
approbation.

For he can fetch and carry, which is patience in
employment.

For he can jump over a stick, which is patience upon
  proof positive.
For he can spraggle upon waggle at the word of
  command.
For he can jump from an eminence into his master's
  bosom.
For he can catch the cork and toss it again.
For he is hated by the hypocrite and miser.
For the former is affraid of detection.
For the latter refuses the charge.
For he camels his back to bear the first notion of
  business.
For he is good to think on, if a man would express
  himself neatly.
For he made a great figure in Egypt for his signal
  services.
For he killed the Icneumon-rat very pernicious by land.
For his ears are so acute that they sting again.
For from this proceeds the passing quickness of his
  attention.
For by stroaking of him I have found out electricity.
For I perceived God's light about him both wax
  and fire.
For the Electrical fire is the spiritual substance, which
  God sends from heaven to sustain the bodies both of
  man and beast.
For God has blessed him in the variety of his
  movements.
For, tho he cannot fly, he is an excellent clamberer.
For his motions upon the face of the earth are more than
  any other quadrupede.
For he can tread to all the measures upon the musick.
For he can swim for life.
For he can creep.

The Stalls of Barchester Cathedral

M. R. James

This matter began, as far as I am concerned, with the reading of a notice in the obituary section of the *Gentleman's Magazine* for an early year in the nineteenth century:

> On February 26th, at his residence in the Cathedral Close of Barchester, the Venerable John Benwell Haynes, D.D., aged 57, Archdeacon of Sowerbridge and Rector of Pickhill and Candley. He was of — College, Cambridge, and where, by talent and assiduity, he commanded the esteem of his seniors; when, at the usual time, he took his first degree, his name stood high in the list of wranglers. These academical honours procured for him within a short time a Fellowship of his College. In the year 1783 he received Holy Orders, and was shortly afterwards presented to the perpetual Curacy of Ranxton-sub-Ashe by his friend and patron the late truly venerable Bishop of Lichfield ... His speedy preferments, first to a Prebend, and subsequently to the dignity of Precentor in the Cathedral of Barchester, form an eloquent testimony to the respect in which he was held and to his eminent qualifications. He succeeded to the Archdeaconry upon the sudden

decease of Archdeacon Pulteney in 1810. His sermons, ever conformable to the principles of the religion and Church which he adorned, displayed in no ordinary degree, without the least trace of enthusiasm, the refinement of the scholar united with the graces of the Christian. Free from sectarian violence, and informed by the spirit of the truest charity, they will long dwell in the memories of his hearers. [Here a further omission.] The productions of his pen include an able defence of Episcopacy, which, though often perused by the author of this tribute to his memory, afford but one additional instance of the want of liberality and enterprise which is a too common characteristic of the publishers of our generation. His published works are, indeed, confined to a spirited and elegant version of the *Argonautica* of Valerius Flaccus, a volume of *Discourses upon the Several Events in the Life of Joshua*, delivered in his Cathedral, and a number of the charges which he pronounced at various visitations to the clergy of his Archdeaconry. These are distinguished by etc., etc. The urbanity and hospitality of the subject of these lines will not readily be forgotten by those who enjoyed his acquaintance. His interest in the venerable and awful pile under whose hoary vault he was so punctual an attendant, and particularly in the musical portion of its rites, might be termed filial, and formed a strong and delightful contrast to the polite indifference displayed by too many of our Cathedral dignitaries at the present time.

The final paragraph, after informing us that Dr Haynes died a bachelor, says:

It might have been augured that an existence so placid and benevolent would have been terminated in a ripe old age by a dissolution equally gradual and calm. But how unsearchable are the workings of Providence! The peaceful and retired seclusion amid which the honoured evening of Dr Haynes's life was mellowing to its close was destined to be disturbed, nay, shattered, by a tragedy as appalling as it was unexpected. The morning of the 26th of February –

But perhaps I shall do better to keep back the remainder of the narrative until I have told the circumstances which led up to it. These, as far as they are now accessible, I have derived from another source.

I had read the obituary notice which I have been quoting, quite by chance, along with a great many others of the same period. It had excited some little speculation in my mind, but, beyond thinking that, if I ever had an opportunity of examining the local records of the period indicated, I would try to remember Dr Haynes, I made no effort to pursue his case.

Quite lately I was cataloguing the manuscripts in the library of the college to which he belonged. I had reached the end of the numbered volumes on the shelves, and I proceeded to ask the librarian whether there were any more books which he thought I ought to include in my description. 'I don't think there are,' he said, 'but we had better come and look at the manuscript class and make sure. Have you time to do that now?' I had time. We went to the library, checked off the manuscripts, and, at the end of our survey, arrived at a shelf of which I had seen nothing. Its contents consisted for the most part of sermons, bundles of fragmentary papers, college exercises, *Cyrus*, an epic poem in several cantos, the product of a country clergyman's leisure, mathematical tracts by a deceased professor, and other similar material of a kind with which I am only too familiar. I took brief notes of these. Lastly, there was a tin box, which was pulled out and dusted. Its label, much faded, was thus inscribed: 'Papers of the Ven. Archdeacon Haynes. Bequeathed in 1834 by his sister, Miss Letitia Haynes.'

I knew at once that the name was one which I had somewhere encountered, and could very soon locate it. 'That must be the Archdeacon Haynes who came to a very odd end at Barchester. I've read his obituary in the *Gentleman's Magazine*. May I take the box home? Do you know if there is anything interesting in it?'

The librarian was very willing that I should take the box and examine it at leisure. 'I never looked inside it myself,' he said, 'but I've always been meaning to. I am pretty sure that is the box which our old Master once said ought never to have been accepted by the college. He said that to Martin years ago; and he said also that as long as he had control over the library it should never be opened. Martin told me about it, and said that he wanted terribly to know what was in it; but the Master was librarian, and always kept the box in the lodge, so there was no getting at it in his time, and when he died it was taken away by mistake by his heirs, and only returned a few years ago. I can't think why I haven't opened it; but, as I have to go away from Cambridge this afternoon, you had better have first go at it. I think I can trust you not to publish anything undesirable in our catalogue.'

I took the box home and examined its contents, and thereafter consulted the librarian as to what should be done about publication, and, since I have his leave to make a story out of it, provided I disguise the identity of the people concerned, I will try what can be done.

The materials are, of course, mainly journals and letters. How much I shall quote and how much epitomise must be determined by considerations of space. The proper understanding of the situation has necessitated a little – not very arduous – research, which has been greatly facilitated by the excellent illustrations and text of the Barchester volume in Bell's *Cathedral Series*.

When you enter the choir of Barchester Cathedral now, you pass through a screen of metal and coloured marbles, designed by Sir Gilbert Scott, and find yourself in what I must call a very bare and odiously furnished place. The stalls are modern, without canopies. The places of the dignitaries and the names of the prebends have fortunately been allowed to survive, and are inscribed on small brass plates affixed to the stalls. The organ is in the triforium, and what is seen of the case is Gothic. The reredos and its surroundings are like every other.

Careful engravings of a hundred years ago show a very different state of things. The organ is on a massive classical screen. The stalls are also classical and very massive. There is a baldacchino of wood over the altar, with urns upon its corners. Farther east is a solid altar screen, classical in design, of wood, with a pediment, in which is a triangle surrounded by rays, enclosing certain Hebrew letters in gold. Cherubs contemplate these. There is a pulpit with a great sounding-board at the eastern end of the stalls on the north side, and there is a black and white marble pavement. Two ladies and a gentleman are admiring the general effect. From other sources I gather that the archdeacon's stall then, as now, was next to the bishop's throne at the south-eastern end of the stalls. His house almost faces the west front of the church, and is a fine red-brick building of William the Third's time.

Here Dr Haynes, already a mature man, took up his abode with his sister in the year 1810. The dignity had long been the object of his wishes, but his predecessor refused to depart until he had attained the age of ninety-two. About a week after he had held a modest festival in celebration of that ninety-second birthday, there came a morning, late in the year, when Dr Haynes, hurrying cheerfully into his breakfast-room, rubbing his hands and humming a tune, was greeted, and checked in his genial flow of spirits, by the sight of his sister, seated, indeed, in her usual place behind the tea-urn, but bowed forward and sobbing unrestrainedly into her handkerchief. 'What – what is the matter? What bad news?' he began.

'Oh, Johnny, you've not heard? The poor dear archdeacon!'

'The archdeacon, yes? What is it – ill, is he?'

'No, no; they found him on the staircase this morning; it is so shocking.'

'Is it possible? Dear, dear, poor Pulteney! Had there been any seizure?'

'They don't think so, and that is almost the worst thing about it. It seems to have been all the fault of that stupid maid of theirs, Jane.'

Dr Haynes paused. 'I don't quite understand, Letitia. How was the maid at fault?'

'Why, as far as I can make out, there was a stair-rod missing, and she never mentioned it, and the poor archdeacon set his foot quite on the edge of the step – you know how slippery that oak is – and it seems he must have fallen almost the whole flight and broken his neck. It is so sad for poor Miss Pulteney. Of course, they will get rid of the girl at once. I never liked her.'

Miss Haynes's grief resumed its sway, but eventually relaxed so far as to permit of her taking some breakfast. Not so her brother, who, after standing in silence before the window for some minutes, left the room, and did not appear again that morning.

I need only add that the careless maid-servant was dismissed forthwith, but that the missing stair-rod was very shortly afterwards found *under* the stair-carpet — an additional proof, if any were needed, of extreme stupidity and carelessness on her part.

For a good many years Dr Haynes had been marked out by his ability, which seems to have been really considerable, as the likely successor of Archdeacon Pulteney, and no disappointment was in store for him. He was duly installed, and entered with zeal upon the discharge of those functions which are appropriate to one in his position. A considerable space in his journals is occupied with exclamations upon the confusion in which Archdeacon Pulteney had left the business of his office and the documents appertaining to it. Dues upon Wringham and Barnswood have been uncollected for something like twelve years, and are largely irrecoverable; no visitation has been held for seven years; four chancels are almost past mending. The persons deputised by the archdeacon have been nearly as incapable as himself. It was almost a matter for thankfulness that this state of things had not been permitted to continue, and a letter from a friend confirms this view. '*ὁ χατεχων*', it says (in rather cruel allusion to the Second Epistle to the Thessalonians), 'is removed at last. My poor friend! Upon what a scene of confusion will you be entering! I give you my word that, on the last occasion of my crossing his threshold, there was no single paper that he could lay hands upon, no syllable of mine that he could hear, and no fact in connection with my business that he could remember. But now, thanks to a negligent maid and a loose stair-carpet, there is some prospect that necessary business will be transacted without a complete loss alike of voice and temper.' This letter was tucked into a pocket in the cover of one of the diaries.

There can be no doubt of the new archdeacon's zeal

and enthusiasm. 'Give me but time to reduce to some semblance of order the innumerable errors and complications with which I am confronted, and I shall gladly and sincerely join with the aged Israelite in the canticle which too many, I fear, pronounce but with their lips.' This reflection I find, not in a diary, but a letter; the doctor's friends seem to have returned his correspondence to his surviving sister. He does not confine himself, however, to reflections. His investigation of the rights and duties of his office are very searching and business-like, and there is a calculation in one place that a period of three years will just suffice to set the business of the Archdeaconry upon a proper footing. The estimate appears to have been an exact one. For just three years he is occupied in reforms; but I look in vain at the end of that time for the promised *Nunc dimittis*. He has now found a new sphere of activity. Hitherto his duties have precluded him from more than an occasional attendance at the Cathedral services. Now he begins to take an interest in the fabric and the music. Upon his struggles with the organist, an old gentleman who had been in office since 1786, I have no time to dwell; they were not attended with any marked success. More to the purpose is his sudden growth of enthusiasm for the Cathedral itself and its furniture. There is a draft of a letter to Sylvanus Urban (which I do not think was ever sent) describing the stalls in the choir. As I have said, these were of fairly late date – of about the year 1700, in fact.

The archdeacon's stall, situated at the south-east end, west of the episcopal throne (now so worthily occupied by the truly excellent prelate who adorns the See of Barchester), is distinguished by some curious ornamentation. In addition to the arms of Dean West,

72

by whose efforts the whole of the internal furniture of the choir was completed, the prayer-desk is terminated at the eastern extremity by three small but remarkable statuettes in the grotesque manner. One is an exquisitely modelled figure of a cat, whose crouching posture suggests with admirable spirit the suppleness, vigilance, and craft of the redoubted adversary of the genus *Mus*. Opposite to this is a figure seated upon a throne and invested with the attributes of royalty; but it is no earthly monarch whom the carver has sought to portray. His feet are studiously concealed by the long robe in which he is draped: but neither the crown nor the cap which he wears suffice to hide the prick-ears and curving horns which betray his Tartarean origin; and the hand which rests upon his knee is armed with talons of horrifying length and sharpness. Between these two figures stands a shape muffled in a long mantle. This might at first sight be mistaken for a monk or 'friar of orders gray', for the head is cowled and a knotted cord depends from somewhere about the waist. A slight inspection, however, will lead to a very different conclusion. The knotted cord is quickly seen to be a halter, held by a hand all but concealed within the draperies; while the sunken features and, horrid to relate, the rent flesh upon the cheek-bones, proclaim the King of Terrors. These figures are evidently the production of no unskilled chisel; and should it chance that any of your correspondents are able to throw light upon their origin and significance, my obligations to your valuable miscellany will be largely increased.

There is more description in the paper, and, seeing that the woodwork in question has now disappeared, it has a considerable interest. A paragraph at the end is worth quoting:

Some late researches among the Chapter accounts have shown me that the carving of the stalls was not, as was very usually reported, the work of Dutch artists, but was executed by a native of this city or district named Austin. The timber was procured from an oak copse in the vicinity, the property of the Dean and Chapter, known as Holywood. Upon a recent visit to the parish within whose boundaries it is situated, I learned from the aged and truly respectable incumbent that traditions still lingered amongst the inhabitants of the great size and age of the oaks employed to furnish the materials of the stately structure which has been, however imperfectly, described in the above lines. Of one in particular, which stood near the centre of the grove, it is remembered that it was known as the Hanging Oak. The propriety of that title is confirmed by the fact that a quantity of human bones was found in the soil about its roots, and that at certain times of the year it was the custom for those who wished to secure a successful issue to their affairs, whether of love or the ordinary business of life, to suspend from its boughs small images or puppets rudely fashioned of straw, twigs, or the like rustic materials.

So much for the archdeacon's archaeological investigations. To return to his career as it is to be gathered from his diaries. Those of his first three years of hard and careful work show him throughout in high spirits, and, doubtless, during this time, that reputation for hospitality and urbanity which is mentioned in his obituary notice was well deserved. After that, as time goes on, I see a shadow coming over him – destined to develop into utter blackness – which I cannot but think must have been reflected in his outward demeanour. He commits a good deal of his fears and troubles to his diary; there was no other outlet for them. He was unmarried, and his sister was not always with him. But I am much mistaken if he has told all that he might have told. A series of extracts shall be given:

Aug. 30, 1816. The days begin to draw in more perceptibly than ever. Now that the Archdeaconry papers are reduced to order, I must find some further employment for the evening hours of autumn and winter. It is a great blow that Letitia's health will not allow her to stay through these months. Why not go on with my *Defence of Episcopacy*? It may be useful.

Sept. 15. Letitia has left me for Brighton.

Oct. 11. Candles lit in the choir for the first time at evening prayers. It came as a shock: I find that I absolutely shrink from the dark season.

Nov. 17. Much struck by the character of the carving on my desk: I do not know that I had ever carefully noticed it before. My attention was called to it by an accident. During the *Magnificat* I was, I regret to say, almost overcome with sleep. My hand was resting on the back of the carved figure of a cat which is the nearest to me of the three figures on the end of my stall. I was not aware of this, for I was not looking in that direction, until I was startled by what seemed a softness, a feeling as of rather rough and coarse fur, and a sudden movement, as if the creature were twisting round its head to bite me. I regained complete consciousness in an instant, and I have some idea that

I must have uttered a suppressed exclamation, for I noticed that Mr Treasurer turned his head quickly in my direction. The impression of the unpleasant feeling was so strong that I found myself rubbing my hand upon my surplice. This accident led me to examine the figures after prayers more carefully than I had done before, and I realised for the first time with what skill they are executed.

Dec. 6. I do indeed miss Letitia's company. The evenings, after I have worked as long as I can at my *Defence*, are very trying. The house is too large for a lonely man, and visitors of any kind are too rare. I get an uncomfortable impression when going to my room that there is company of some kind. The fact is (I may as well formulate it to myself) that I hear voices. This, I am well aware, is a common symptom of incipient decay of the brain – and I believe that I should be less disquieted than I am if I had any suspicion that this was the cause. I have none – none whatever, nor is there anything in my family history to give colour to such an idea. Work, diligent work, and a punctual attention to the duties which fall to me is my best remedy, and I have little doubt that it will prove efficacious.

Jan. 1. My trouble is, I must confess it, increasing upon me. Last night, upon my return after midnight from the Deanery, I lit my candle to go upstairs. I was nearly at the top when something whispered to me, 'Let me wish you a happy New Year.' I could not be mistaken: it spoke distinctly and with a peculiar emphasis. Had I dropped my candle, as I all but did, I tremble to think what the consequences must have been. As it was, I managed to get up the last flight, and was quickly in my room with the door locked, and experienced no other disturbance.

Jan. 15. I had occasion to come downstairs last night to my workroom for my watch, which I had inadvertently left on my table when I went up to bed. I think I was at the top of the last flight when I had a sudden impression of a sharp whisper in my ear: '*Take care.*' I clutched the balusters and naturally looked round at once. Of course, there was nothing. After a moment I went on – it was no good turning back – but I had as nearly as possible fallen: a cat – a large one by the feel of it – slipped between my feet, but again, of course, I saw nothing. It *may* have been the kitchen cat, but I do not think it was.

Feb. 27. A curious thing last night, which I should like to forget. Perhaps if I put it down here I may see it in its true proportion. I worked in the library from about nine to ten. The hall and staircase seemed to be unusually full of what I can only call movement without sound: by this I mean that there seemed to be continuous going and coming, and that whenever I ceased writing to listen, or looked out into the hall, the stillness was absolutely unbroken. Nor, in going to my room at an earlier hour than usual – about half past ten – was I conscious of anything that I could call a noise. It so happened that I had told John to come to my room for the letter to the bishop which I wished to have delivered early in the morning at the Palace. He was to sit up, therefore, and come for it when he heard me retire. This I had for the moment forgotten, though I had remembered to carry the letter with me to my room. But when, as I was winding up my watch, I heard a light tap at the door, and a low voice saying, 'May I come in?' (which I most undoubtedly did hear),

I recollected the fact, and took up the letter from my dressing-table, saying, 'Certainly: come in.' No one, however, answered my summons, and it was now that, as I strongly suspect, I committed an error: for I opened the door and held the letter out. There was certainly no one at that moment in the passage, but, in the instant of my standing there, the door at the end opened and John appeared carrying a candle. I asked him whether he had come to the door earlier; but am satisfied that he had not. I do not like the situation; but although my senses were very much on the alert, and though it was some time before I could sleep, I must allow that I perceived nothing further of an untoward character.

With the return of spring, when his sister came to live with him for some months, Dr Haynes's entries become more cheerful, and, indeed, no symptom of depression is discernible until the early part of September, when he was again left alone. And now, indeed, there is evidence that he was incommoded again, and that more pressingly. To this matter I will return in a moment, but I digress to put in a document which, rightly or wrongly, I believe to have a bearing on the thread of the story.

The account-books of Dr Haynes, preserved along with his other papers, show, from a date but little later than that of his institution as archdeacon, a quarterly payment of £25 to 'J. L.'. Nothing could have been made of this, had it stood by itself. But I connect with it a very dirty and ill-written letter, which, like another that I have quoted, was in a pocket in the cover of a diary. Of date or postmark there is no vestige, and the decipherment was not easy. It appears to run:

Dr Sr.

I have bin expctin to her off you theis last wicks, and not Haveing done so must supose you have not got mine witch was saying how me and my man had met in with bad times this season all seems to go cross with us on the farm and which way to look for the rent we have no knowledge of it this been the sad case with us if you would have the great [liberality *probably, but the exact spelling defies reproduction*] to send fourty pounds otherwise steps will have to be took which I should not wish. Has you was the Means of me losing my place with Dr Pulteney I think it is only just what I am asking and you know best what I could say if I was Put to it but I do not wish anything of that unpleasant Nature being one that always wish to have everything Pleasant about me.

Your obedt Servt,

JANE LEE.

About the time at which I suppose this letter to have been written there is, in fact, a payment of £40 to J. L.

We return to the diary:

Oct. 22. At evening prayers, during the Psalms, I had that same experience which I recollect from last year. I was resting my hand on one of the carved figures, as before (I usually avoid that of the cat now), and − I was going to have said − a change came over it, but that seems attributing too much importance to what must, after all, be due to some physical affection in myself: at any rate, the wood seemed to become chilly and soft as if made of wet linen. I can assign the moment at which I became sensible of this. The choir were singing the words [*Set thou an ungodly man to be ruler over him and*] let Satan stand at *his right hand.*

The whispering in my house was more persistent tonight. I seemed not to be rid of it in my room. I have not noticed this before. A nervous man, which I am not, and hope I am not becoming, would have been much annoyed, if not alarmed, by it. The cat was on the stairs tonight. I think it sits there always. There is no kitchen cat.

Nov. 15. Here again I must note a matter I do not understand. I am much troubled in sleep. No definite image presented itself, but I was pursued by the very vivid impression that wet lips were whispering into my ear with great rapidity and emphasis for some time together. After this, I suppose, I fell asleep, but was awakened with a start by a feeling as if a hand were laid on my shoulder. To my intense alarm I found myself standing at the top of the lowest flight of the first staircase. The moon was shining brightly enough through the large window to let me see that there was a large cat on the second or third step. I can make no comment. I crept up to bed again, I do not know how. Yes, mine is a heavy burden. [Then follows a line or two which has been scratched out. I fancy I read something like 'acted for the best'.]

Not long after this it is evident to me that the archdeacon's firmness began to give way under the pressure of these phenomena. I omit as unnecessarily painful and distressing the ejaculations and prayers which, in the months of December and January, appear for the first time and become increasingly frequent. Throughout this time, however, he is obstinate in clinging to his post. Why he did not plead ill-health and take refuge at Bath or Brighton I cannot tell; my impression is that it would have done him no good; that he was a man who, if he had confessed himself beaten by the annoyances, would have succumbed at once, and that he was conscious of this. He did seek to palliate them by inviting visitors to his house. The result he has noted in this fashion:

Jan. 7. I have prevailed on my cousin Allen to give me a few days, and he is to occupy the chamber next to mine.

Jan. 8. A still night. Allen slept well, but complained of the wind. My own experiences were as before: still whispering and whispering: what is it that he wants to say?

Jan. 9. Allen thinks this a very noisy house. He thinks, too, that my cat is an unusually large and fine specimen, but very wild.

Jan. 10. Allen and I in the library until 11. He left me twice to see what the maids were doing in the hall: returning the second time he told me he had seen one of them passing through the door at the end of the passage, and said if his wife were here she would soon get them into better order. I asked him what coloured dress the maid wore; he said grey or white. I supposed it would be so.

Jan. 11. Allen left me today. I must be firm.

These words, *I must be firm*, occur again and again on subsequent days; sometimes they are the only entry. In these cases they are in an unusually large hand, and dug into the paper in a way which must have broken the pen that wrote them.

Apparently the archdeacon's friends did not remark any change in his behaviour, and this gives me a high idea of his courage and determination. The diary tells us nothing more than I have indicated of the last days of his life. The end of it all must be told in the polished language of the obituary notice:

The morning of the 26th of February was cold and tempestuous. At an early hour the servants had occasion to go into the front hall of the residence occupied by the lamented subject of these lines. What was their horror upon observing the form of their beloved and respected master lying upon the landing of the principal staircase in an attitude which inspired the gravest fears. Assistance was procured, and an universal consternation was experienced upon the discovery that he had been the object of a brutal and a murderous attack. The vertebral column was fractured in more than one place. This might have been the result of a fall: it appeared that the stair-carpet was loosened at one point. But, in addition to this, there were injuries inflicted upon the eyes, nose and mouth, as if by the agency of some savage animal, which, dreadful to relate, rendered those features unrecognisable. The vital spark was, it is needless to add, completely extinct, and had been so, upon the testimony of respectable medical authorities, for several hours. The author or authors of this mysterious outrage are alike buried in mystery, and the most active conjecture has hitherto failed to suggest a solution of the melancholy problem afforded by this appalling occurrence.

The writer goes on to reflect upon the probability

that the writings of Mr Shelley, Lord Byron, and M. Voltaire may have been instrumental in bringing about the disaster, and concludes by hoping, somewhat vaguely, that this event may 'operate as an example to the rising generation'; but this portion of his remarks need not be quoted in full.

I had already formed the conclusion that Dr Haynes was responsible for the death of Dr Pulteney. But the incident connected with the carved figure of death upon the archdeacon's stall was a very perplexing feature. The conjecture that it had been cut out of the wood of the Hanging Oak was not difficult, but seemed impossible to substantiate. However, I paid a visit to Barchester, partly with the view of finding out whether there were any relics of the woodwork to be heard of. I was introduced by one of the canons to the curator of the local museum, who was, my friend said, more likely to be able to give me information on the point than anyone else. I told this gentleman of the description of certain carved figures and arms formerly on the stalls, and asked whether any had survived. He was able to show me the arms of Dean West and some other fragments. These, he said, had been got from an old resident, who had also once owned a figure – perhaps one of those which I was inquiring for. There was a very odd thing about that figure, he said. 'The old man who had it told me that he picked it up in a wood-yard, whence he had obtained the still extant pieces, and had taken it home for his children. On the way home he was fiddling about with it and it came in two in his hands, and a bit of paper dropped out. This he picked up and, just noticing that there was writing on it, put it into his pocket, and subsequently into a vase on his mantelpiece. I was at his house not very long ago, and happened to pick up the vase and turn it over to see whether there were any marks on it, and the paper fell into my hand. The old man, on my handing it to him, told me the story I have told you, and said I might keep the paper. It was crumpled and rather torn, so I have mounted it on a card, which I have here. If you can tell me what it means I shall be very glad, and also, I may say, a good deal surprised.'

He gave me the card. The paper was quite legibly inscribed in an old hand, and this is what was on it:

> When I grew in the Wood
> I was water'd wth Blood
> Now in the Church I stand
> Who that touches me with his Hand
> If a Bloody hand he bear
> I councell him to be ware
> Lest he be fetcht away
> Whether by night or day,
> But chiefly when the wind blows high
> In a night of February.

This I drempt, 26 Febr. A° 1699. JOHN AUSTIN.

'I suppose it is a charm or a spell: wouldn't you call it something of that kind?' said the curator.

'Yes,' I said, 'I suppose one might. What became of the figure in which it was concealed?'

'Oh, I forgot,' said he. 'The old man told me it was so ugly and frightened his children so much that he burnt it.'

The Parson and the Cat *

'William Cowper Junior' (Rev. James Everett)

Let Cowper's ease and merry vein,
   In every verse appear,
And soon shall Nimrod's cassock'd train
   To Gilpin tune the ear.

'Twas at a time when scent was keen,
   What dog his nose could blame?
A Vicar paced the sylvan scene,
   In hot pursuit of game.

Only more strong the burning scent,
   When livings were in view;
The fleece possess'd, – he lived content,
   Though vacant every pew.

---

*Reverend James Everett (1734–1872), who wrote this poem under the pseudonym William Cowper Junior because of its debt to 'John Gilpin', was a Weslyan Methodist minister as well as a bookseller and scholar. (His attack in this 'serio-comic satirical poem' of *c.* 1820 is not only on hunting parsons but also on those who heat churches and play organ music.)

More fragrant far such scent inhaled,
   Than incense upward borne,
No psalmody his ears assailed,
   Like clang of huntsman's horn.

Dearer to him the pack's full cry,
   Than Sabbath-bell's deep tone;
Not half so sweet the sinner's sigh,
   As Reynard's dying groan.

He saw a swain as forth he hied,
   Advancing to a brook,
Whose cat beneath his arm was tied,
   With wildness in her look.

'And whither,' asked the buckskin priest,
   'Say, whither dost thou go?
If silent here, – relate at least,
   Why bind Miss Pussey so?'

'Why,' said John, 'an't please your honour,
   I go this cat to drown.'
'Why not set the dogs upon her?
   They soon will hunt her down.'

To please his heavenly minded guide,
   Of tenderness composed,
He took poor pussey from his side,
   By hungry dogs enclosed.

And soon he snapp'd her hempen fetters,
   For sport prepared the way, –
Sport, so fitting men of letters,
   Returned to childhood's day.

Full joyous was the priest as pack,
   When John threw down the cat,
The tide of early life roll'd back,
   In spite of wig and hat.

Tho' paid for preaching, – 'twas his choice
   To whisper out the truth:
But now he stretch'd his stentor voice,
   More loud than any youth.

The dogs who knew their patron's shout, –
   Nor did his flock so well,
Fired with parsonic zeal throughout,
   Made echo every dell.

Poor puss, in fright, for mercy begs,
   Nor tree nor mercy near,
She fastens on the horse's legs,
   And mounts him by the rear.

The steed unused to such a guest,
   Still less to spurs behind,
Snorted, and kicked, and onward press'd,
   A resting place to find.

Nor were her fangs the less employed,
   Her safety to complete;
'Twas through their grasp she still enjoyed,
   Her elevated seat.

The angry pack in dread array,
   With widened jaws and thoats,
Leaped round and round the prancing bay,
   Howling their hideous notes.

Through raising fear and lengthened pain,
    The horse still raged the more,
And now, to sit, and guide the rein,
    The rider deemed were o'er.

Off went the parson with his mate,
    The hounds in full pursuit;
Transferr'd to him was her dread fate,
    He now, alas!, was mute.

A change of scene effected thus; –
    The priest appeared the game;
The triumph seemed to rest with puss,
    Till near the trackers came.

At length the ardour of the steed,
    Was checked by strength of arm;
The dog closed in which took the lead,
    And puss was all alarm.

Afraid lest some rude hound should reach,
    And drag her through the pack,
She left the horse's goaded breech,
    And scaled the parson's back.

Around his neck, in apish mood,
    Her foremost limbs she twined,
And from each cheek she drew the blood,
    As erst from steed behind.

Thus author-like, fair EXTRACTS made,
    Not ELEGANT, 'tis true,
But cutting as the sharpest blade,
    And flowing to the view.

Such Extracts from a work so rare –
    A Sportsman and Divine,
Must surely make the reader stare,
    Be doomed for aye to shine.

Himself he could not disengage,
    From pussey's fond embrace;
'Twas toil enough to calm the rage,
    And check the horse's pace.

The howling dogs now thickened round
    All thirsting for the cat;
The hunter made a sudden bound,
    And off flew wig and hat.

Away went priest – away went he,
    Like Gilpin fam'd of yore;
The villagers came out to see,
    The dogs kept up the roar.

Both old and young their voices raised,
    'Our Parson!' was the cry;
To see such game they stood amazed,
    And rent with shouts the sky.

Not long before they saw him borne,
    Full stately to the sight,
But little dreamt so swift return,
    And in such piteous plight.

His cheeks were like the damask rose,
    But not with morning air;
Miss Pussey, with the tint that glows,
    Had placed her pencil there.

All mingled in the merry chace,
    The greatest and the least,
The village cur e'en shewed his face,
    To kennel up the priest.

As forth the hound and human pack
    Poured like a stream along,
Some joined, like minor rills, their track,
    And sung the jocund song.

Again the rider checked his horse,
    And hoped for parish aid,
But noisy crowds made matters worse,
    The steed was more afraid.

Away went priest – away went he,
    Like Gilpin famed of yore;
'Twas laughable Miss Puss to see,
    As high as heretofore.

The seat of learning she had gained,
    Which spoke superior sense,
And though unroofed, she still maintained
    It should not drive her thence.

The time was once – but then had fled,
    When easy had it been,
To deck, with frizzled roof, her head,
    Enlivening thus the scene.

For, in her fear, she might have placed,
    Her head beneath the wig,
And, forcing upward, might in haste
    Have run another rig.

One sudden spring, when on the rise,
    Had borne it off complete;
With hat and wig, – how wondrous wise!
    So near to learning's seat.

Ah, luckless wight, he should have been
    Within his study walls,
Where seldom such as he are seen,
    Though loud the church's calls.

He brought from college his degree,
    But studious habits left;
The scholar's shadow you might see,
    Of substance he was reft.

Preferment's goal he long had gained,
    And fattened on the spoil;
The present goal unseen remained, –
    For this he still must toil.

Miss Pussey like the parson rode,
    And like him kept her hold,
And while she o'er his Reverence strode,
    Each twitch she gave him told.

Her form between his shoulders lay,
    Her head behind his own,
Her foremost limbs were free to play,
    And straight before her thrown.

Her limbs – the rein, her claws – the bit,
    Like tenter hooks to view,
And while she held as seemed her fit,
    His cheeks she backward drew.

The more she drew as moved by fear; –
   If fancy speak the truth,
She nearly stretched from ear to ear,
   His Reverence's mouth.

The neighbouring swains who met him straight,
   Would deem him catching flies,
But soon he passed – they saw his fate,
   When pussey caught their eyes.

Ah! luckless wight, had he but been
   Intent upon his call,
He had not now beheld this scene,
   Nor thus been jeered by all.

But still though greatly out of place,
   For safety he must strive,
Once more he checked his horse's pace,
   To every fear alive.

The roar of dogs and swains was heard,
   And nearer as they came,
More desperate still the steed appeared,
   Nor skill his rage could tame.

Away went priest – away went he,
   Like Gilpin famed of yore;
The fence-crushed farmer said with glee,
   'We ne'er shall see him more.'

Others anon as loudly cried,
   'No fear of him today; –
Far better he is skill'd to ride,
   Than skill'd to preach and pray.'

Let him, some wags might next have said,
    Nor limb nor cranium break;
The goal by him must soon be made,
    Or puss will tithe his cheek.

And why not pay like those around,
    For pleasures thus received?
It matters not how harsh the sound, –
    The tithed are always grieved;

And grieved the more, as tithes are given
    To those whom all declare
Nor either seek the road to heaven,
    Nor point their hearers there.

These are the Church's greatest foes,
    And not the different sects;
From these she feels the heaviest blows,
    On these the muse reflects.

And yet, than drunkards, and the gay,
    Dancers, and stage offenders,
Few talk of 'DANGER' more than they,
    Or plume themselves defenders.

Not on the good, in Heaven's pursuit,
    Who toil with all their power;
But grubs who only eat the fruit,
    Would satire's vengeance shower.

In virtue's cause – whate'er the name,
    The muse would e'er assume
The two-edged sword, – a sword of flame,
    Her enemies to consume,

But stay, while wandering from my tale,
  Wide as the priest from sport,
The painted claws his cheeks assail,
  His features still distort.

The pars'nage-house at length was gained,
  Without a broken limb,
But ne'er was he so tightly reined,
  Nor caught in such a trim.

The house-dog heard the horse's feet,
  And hastened to the door,
His master's reverend eye to meet,
  And greet him as before.

How much surprised to see his lord,
  With mouth so widely stretched!
Though grinning – not an angry word,
  No hand to him was reach'd.

The mastiff knew – for wise was he,
  That he had done no harm,
Nor sooner did Miss Pussey see,
  Than he began to warm,

Forward he dashed in bristled mood;
  The horse again took fright,
But ere he drew a drop of blood,
  The pack was full in sight.

And who his gruffness could gainsay,
  Though with the hounds he fought?
He wished a snack as well as they,
  For this he sternly sought.

Tremendous was the fray indeed,
    And madly did they strive;
The priest, in poor Miss Pussey's stead,
    Was next to flayed alive.

Fancy would sketch another scene, –
    For farming priests abound,
And shew the stack-yard, and the green,
    In motion all around.

The chuckling hens and cackling geese,
    United with the dogs,
Cows, calves & sheep, who sought their peace,
    Fled with the grunting hogs.

Fear, ire, and mirth prevailed throughout,
    Though slight indeed the cause,
For all were moved or put to rout,
    By touch of pussey's claws.

With Hogarth's genius brought to bear,
    On villagers and beasts,
On poultry flying through the air,
    On chief of hunting priests;

Soon would a new creation rise,
    With cat and scampering crowd,
The clerk, to lead, with leering eyes,
    The choristers so loud.

The parson, more than satisfied,
    With leave, we now dismount,
And place both mirth and wounded pride,
    To pussey's just account.

But what can inmates say or do,
    Returning in such haste?
He carries game – Miss Puss, 'tis true, –
    But not to suit the taste.

Enough of her to stay his fast,
    For one fair morning's meal;
He gladly hoped 'twould be the last,
    His appetite should feel.

'Tis but to guess how pussey fared,
    Though guiltless more than he;
For cruel intent, *he* was not spared,
    His friends must e'en agree.

But all may know how he was heard,
    And heard with what applause,
When in the rostrum, he appeared,
    With scars in such a cause.

What merriment would Paul inspire,
    Religion how much slur,
Clothed with huntsman's red attire,
    In boots, and cap, and spur!

How strange to Christian ears the sound
    To come from Peter's lip,
'Hark, hark to cover,' to the hound,
    And see him crack his whip!

In other language than to bless,
    It were outrageous quite;
In other than the priestly dress,
    Unseemly to the sight.

As strange it were to see a pig
   Come bolting from the stye,
With three-cocked hat, and powdered wig,
   Laced coat, and buskins high.

Oh! worse than swine, more useless far,
   And still more out of place,
No more in Christ's right hand, a star,
   A blot on Zion's face, –

Yes, worse, – whose fate we here rehearse,
   And may he stand alone!
May priests no longer shine in verse,
   Where knaves and fools are shown.

Repent, reform, and imitate
   Those clergymen of fame, –
True pillars of the Church and State,
   Of EVANGELIC name;

Those men, whose piety and zeal,
   Put sportsmen to the blush,
Who only toil for Zion's weal,
   And scorn to beat the bush.

This, for the tuneful organ calls,
   To draw the thoughtless crowd,
And *that*, to warm the church's walls,
   For blazing fire is loud.

Thus wide the good man never roves;
   For these ne'er opes his mouth;
He warms his church with *living stoves*,
   He draws by force of TRUTH.

Let every pulpit once be fill'd,
  With EVANGELIC men,
Soon shall the voice of foes be still'd,
  And useless be their pen.

May glorious days the Church await!
  Such glories meet our eyes!
When every pile shall prove too straight,
  And new ones towering rise.

And now we sing God save the King
  And Church from selfish ends;
Pray for ever, Lord deliver
  From Nimrod's cassock'd friends!

The Cat and Cupid

Arnold Bennett

I

The secret history of the Ebag marriage is now printed for the first time. The Ebag family, who prefer their name to be accented on the first syllable, once almost ruled Oldcastle, which is a clean and conceited borough, with long historical traditions, on the very edge of the industrial, democratic and unclean Five Towns. The Ebag family still lives in the grateful memory of Oldcastle, for no family ever did more to preserve the celebrated Oldcastilian superiority in social, moral and religious matters over the vulgar Five Towns. The episodes leading to the Ebag marriage could only have happened in Oldcastle. By which I mean merely that they could not have happened in any of the Five Towns. In the Five Towns that sort of thing does not occur. I don't know why, but it doesn't. The people are too deeply interested in football, starting prices, rates, public parks, sliding scales, excursions to Blackpool, and municipal shindies, to concern themselves with organists as such. In the Five Towns an organist may be a sanitary inspector or an auctioneer on Mondays. In Oldcastle an organist is an organist, recognised as such in the streets. No one ever heard of an organist in the Five Towns being taken up and petted by a couple of old ladies. But this may occur at Oldcastle. It, in fact, did.

The scandalous circumstances which led to the disappearance from the Oldcastle scene of Mr Skerritt, the original organist of St Placid, have no relation to the present narrative, which opens when the ladies Ebag began to seek for a new organist. The new church of St Placid owed its magnificent existence to the Ebag family. The apse had been given entirely by old Caiaphas Ebag (ex-MP, now a paralytic sufferer) at a cost of twelve thousand pounds; and his was the original idea of building the church. When, owing to the decline of the working man's interest in beer, and one or two other things, Caiaphas lost nearly the whole of his fortune, which had been gained by honest labour in mighty speculations, he rather regretted the church; he would have preferred twelve thousand in cash to a view of the apse from his bedroom window; but he was man enough never to complain. He lived, after his misfortunes, in a comparatively small house with his two daughters, Mrs Ebag and Miss Ebag. These two ladies are the heroines of the tale.

Mrs Ebag had married her cousin, who had died. She possessed about six hundred a year of her own. She was two years older than her sister, Miss Ebag, a spinster. Miss Ebag was two years younger than Mrs Ebag. No further information as to their respective ages ever leaked out. Miss Ebag had a little money of her own from her deceased mother, and Caiaphas had the wreck of his riches. The total income of the household was not far short of a thousand a year, but of this quite two hundred a year was absorbed by young Edith Ebag, Mrs Ebag's step-daughter (for Mrs Ebag had been her husband's second choice).

Edith, who was notorious as a silly chit and spent most of her time in London and other absurd places, formed no part of the household, though she visited it occasionally. The household consisted of old Caiaphas, bedridden, and his two daughters and Goldie. Goldie was the tomcat, so termed by reason of his splendid tawniness. Goldie had more to do with the Ebag marriage than anyone or anything, except the weathercock on the top of the house. This may sound queer, but is as naught to the queerness about to be unfolded.

II

It cannot be considered unnatural that Mrs and Miss Ebag, with the assistance of the vicar, should have managed the affairs of the church. People nicknamed them 'the churchwardens', which was not quite nice, having regard to the fact that their sole aim was the truest welfare of the church. They and the vicar, in a friendly and effusive way, hated each other. Sometimes they got the better of the vicar, and, less often, he got the better of them. In the choice of a new organist they won. Their candidate was Mr Carl Ullman, the artistic orphan.

Mr Carl Ullman is the hero of the tale. The son of one of those German designers of earthenware who at intervals come and settle in the Five Towns for the purpose of explaining fully to the inhabitants how inferior England is to Germany, he had an English mother, and he himself was violently English. He spoke English like an Englishman and German like an Englishman. He could paint, model in clay, and play three musical instruments, including the

101

organ. His one failing was that he could never earn enough to live on. It seemed as if he was always being drawn by an invisible string towards the workhouse door. Now and then he made half a sovereign extra by deputising on the organ. In such manner had he been introduced to the Ebag ladies. His romantic and gloomy appearance had attracted them, with the result that they had asked him to lunch after the service, and he had remained with them till the evening service. During the visit they had learnt that his grandfather had been Court Councillor in the Kingdom of Saxony. Afterwards they often said to each other how ideal it would be if only Mr Skerritt might be removed and Carl Ullman take his place. And when Mr Skerritt actually was removed, by his own wickedness, they regarded it as almost an answer to prayer, and successfully employed their powerful interest on behalf of Carl. The salary was a hundred a year. Not once in his life had Carl earned a hundred pounds in a single year. For him the situation meant opulence. He accepted it, but calmly, gloomily. Romantic gloom was his joy in life. He said with deep melancholy that he was sure he could not find a convenient lodging in Oldcastle. And the ladies Ebag then said that he must really come and spend a few days with them and Goldie and Papa until he was 'suited'. He said that he hated to plant himself on people, and yielded to the request. The ladies Ebag fussed around his dark-eyed and tranquil pessimism, and both of them instantly grew younger – a curious but authentic phenomenon. They adored his playing, and they were enchanted to discover that his notions about hymn tunes agreed with theirs, and by consequence disagreed with the vicar's. In the first week or two they scored off the vicar five times, and the advantage of having your organist in your own house grew very apparent. They were also greatly impressed by his gentleness with Goldie and by his intelligent interest in serious questions.

One day Miss Ebag said timidly to her sister: 'It's just six months today.'

'What do you mean, sister?' asked Mrs Ebag, self-consciously.

'Since Mr Ullman came.'

'So it is!' said Mrs Ebag, who was just as well aware of the date as the spinster was aware of it.

They said no more. The position was the least bit delicate. Carl had found no lodging. He did not offer to go. They did not want him to go. He did not offer to pay. And really he cost them nothing except laundry, whisky and fussing. How could they suggest that he should pay? He lived amidst them like a beautiful mystery, and all were seemingly content. Carl was probably saving the whole of his salary, for he never bought clothes and he did not smoke. The ladies Ebag simply did what they liked about hymn tunes.

III

You would have thought that no outsider would find a word to say, and you would have been mistaken. The fact that Mrs Ebag was two years older than Miss and Miss two years younger than Mrs Ebag; the fact that old Caiaphas was, for strong reasons, always in the house; the fact that the ladies were notorious cat-idolaters; the fact that the reputation of the Ebag family was and had ever been spotless; the fact that the Ebag family had given the apse and practically created the entire church; all these facts added together did not prevent the outsider from finding a word to say.

At first words were not said; but looks were looked, and coughs were coughed. Then someone, strolling into the church of a morning while Carl Ullman was practising, saw Miss Ebag sitting in silent ecstasy in a corner. And a few mornings later the same someone, whose curiosity had been excited, veritably saw Mrs Ebag in the organ-loft with Carl Ullman, but no sign of Miss Ebag. It was at this juncture that words began to be said.

Words! Not complete sentences! The sentences were never finished. 'Of course, it's no affair of mine, but –' 'I wonder that people like the Ebags should –' 'Not that I should ever dream of hinting that –' 'First one and then the other – well!' 'I'm sure that if either Mrs or Miss Ebag had the slightest idea they'd at once –' And so on. Intangible gossamer criticism, floating in the air!

IV

One evening – it was precisely the first of June – when a thunderstorm was blowing up from the south-west, and scattering the smoke of the Five Towns to the four corners of the world, and making the weathercock of the house of the Ebags creak, the ladies Ebag and Carl Ullman sat together as usual in the drawing-room. The french window was open, but banged to at intervals. Carl Ullman had played the piano and the ladies Ebag – Mrs Ebag, somewhat comfortably stout and Miss Ebag spare – were talking very well and sensibly about the influence of music on character. They invariably chose such subjects for conversation. Carl was chiefly silent, but now and then, after a sip of whisky, he would say, 'Yes,' with impressiveness and stare gloomily out of the darkening window. The ladies Ebag had a remarkable example of the influence of music on character in the person of Edith Ebag. It appeared that Edith would never play anything but waltzes – Waldteufel's for choice – and that the foolish frivolity of her flyaway character was a direct consequence of this habit. Carl felt sadly glad, after hearing the description of Edith's carryings-on, that Edith had chosen to live far away.

And then the conversation languished and died with the daylight, and a certain self-consciousness obscured the social atmosphere. For a vague rumour of the chatter of the town had penetrated the house, and the ladies Ebag, though they scorned chatter, were affected by it; Carl Ullman, too. It had the customary effect of such chatter; it fixed the thoughts of those chatted about on matters which perhaps would not otherwise have occupied their attention.

The ladies Ebag said to themselves: 'We are no longer aged nineteen. We are moreover living with our father. If he is bedridden, what then? This gossip connecting our names with that of Mr Ullman is worse than baseless; it is preposterous. We assert positively that we have no designs of any kind on Mr Ullman.'

Nevertheless, by dint of thinking about that gossip, the naked idea of a marriage with Mr Ullman soon ceased to shock them. They could gaze at it without going into hysterics.

As for Carl, he often meditated upon his own age, which might have been anything between thirty and forty-five, and upon the mysterious ages of the ladies, and upon their goodness, their charm, their seriousness, their intelligence and their sympathy with himself.

Hence the self-consciousness in the gloaming.

To create a diversion Miss Ebag walked primly to the window and cried:

'Goldie! Goldie!'

It was Goldie's bedtime. In summer he always strolled into the garden after dinner, and he nearly always sensibly responded to the call when his bed-hour sounded. No one would have dreamed of retiring until Goldie was safely ensconced in his large basket under the stairs.

'Naughty Goldie!' Miss Ebag said, comprehensively, to the garden.

She went into the garden to search, and Mrs Ebag followed her, and Carl Ullman followed Mrs Ebag. And they searched without result, until it was black night and the threatening storm at last fell. The vision of Goldie out in that storm desolated the ladies, and Carl Ullman displayed the nicest feeling. At length the rain drove them in and they stood in the drawing-room with anxious faces, while two servants, under directions from Carl, searched the house for Goldie.

'If you please'm,' stammered the housemaid, rushing rather unconventionally into the drawing-room, 'Cook says she thinks Goldie must be on the roof, in the vane.'

'On the roof in the vane?' exclaimed Mrs Ebag, pale. 'In the vane?'

'Yes'm.'

'Whatever do you mean, Sarah?' asked Miss Ebag, even paler.

The ladies Ebag were utterly convinced that Goldie was not like other cats, that he never went on the roof, that he never had any wish to do anything that was not in the strictest sense gentlemanly and correct. And if by chance he did go on the roof, it was merely to examine the roof itself, or to enjoy the view therefrom out of gentlemanly curiosity. So that this reference to the roof shocked them. The night did not favour the theory of view-gazing.

'Cook says she heard the weather-vane creaking ever since she went upstairs after dinner, and now it's stopped; and she can hear Goldie a-myowling like anything.'

'Is Cook in her attic?' asked Mrs Ebag.

'Yes'm.'

'Ask her to come out. Mr Ullman, will you be so very good as to come upstairs and investigate?'

Cook, enveloped in a cloak, stood out on the second landing, while Mr Ullman and the ladies invaded her chamber. The noise of myowling was terrible. Mr Ullman opened the dormer window, and the rain burst in, together with a fury of myowling. But he did not care. It lightened and thundered. But he did not care. He procured a chair of Cook's and put it under the window and stood on it, with his back to the window, and twisted forth his body so that he could spy up the roof. The ladies protested that he would be wet through, but he paid no heed to them.

Then his head, dripping, returned into the room.

'I've just seen by a flash of lightning,' he said in a voice of emotion. 'The poor animal has got his tail fast in the socket of the weather-vane. He must have been whisking it about up there, and the vane turned and caught it. The vane is jammed.'

'How dreadful!' said Mrs Ebag. 'Whatever can be done?'

'He'll be dead before morning,' sobbed Miss Ebag.

'I shall climb up the roof and release him,' said Carl Ullman, gravely.

They forbade him to do so. Then they implored him to refrain. But he was adamant. And in their supplications there was a note of insincerity, for their hearts bled for Goldie, and, further, they were not altogether unwilling that Carl should prove himself a hero. And so, amid apprehensive feminine cries of the acuteness of his danger, Carl crawled out of the window and faced the thunder, the lightning, the rain, the slippery roof, and the maddened cat. A group of three servants were huddled outside the attic door.

In the attic the ladies could hear his movements on the roof, moving higher and higher. The suspense was extreme. Then there was silence; even the myowling had ceased. Then a clap of thunder; and then, after that, a terrific clatter on the roof, a bounding downwards as of a great stone, a curse, a horrid pause, and finally a terrific smashing of foliage and cracking of wood.

Mrs Ebag sprang to the window.

'It's all right,' came a calm, gloomy voice from below. 'I fell into the rhododendrons, and Goldie followed me. I'm not hurt, thank goodness! Just my luck!'

A bell rang imperiously. It was the paralytic's bell. He had been disturbed by these unaccustomed phenomena.

'Sister, do go to Father at once,' said Mrs Ebag, as they both hastened downstairs in a state of emotion, assuredly unique in their lives.

V

Mrs Ebag met Carl and the cat as they dripped into the gas-lit drawing-room. They presented a surprising spectacle, and they were doing damage to the Persian carpet at the rate of about five shillings a second; but that Carl, and the beloved creature for whom he had dared so much, were equally unhurt appeared to be indubitable. Of course, it was a miracle. It could not be regarded as other than a miracle.

Mrs Ebag gave vent to an exclamation in which were mingled pity, pride, admiration and solicitude, and then remained, as it were, spellbound. The cat escaped from those protecting arms and fled away. Instead of following Goldie, Mrs Ebag continued to gaze at the hero.

'How can I thank you!' she whispered.

'What for?' asked Carl, with laconic gloom.

'For having saved my darling!' said Mrs Ebag. And there was passion in her voice.

'Oh!' said Carl. 'It was nothing!'

'Nothing?' Mrs Ebag repeated after him, with melting eyes, as if to imply that, instead of being nothing, it was everything; as if to imply that his deed must rank hereafter with the most splendid deeds of antiquity; as if to imply that the whole affair was beyond words to utter or gratitude to repay.

And in fact Carl himself was moved. You cannot fall from the roof of a two-storey house into a very high-class rhododendron bush, carrying a prize cat in your arms, without being a bit shaken. And Carl was a bit shaken, not merely physically, but morally and spiritually. He could not deny to himself that he had after all done something rather wondrous, which ought to be celebrated in sounding verse. He felt that he was in an atmosphere far removed from the commonplace.

He dripped steadily on to the carpet.

'You know how dear my cat was to me,' proceeded Mrs Ebag. 'And you risked your life to spare me the pain of his suffering, perhaps his death. How thankful I am that I insisted on having those rhododendrons planted just where they are – fifteen years ago! I never anticipated –'

She stopped. Tears came into her dowager eyes. It was obvious that she worshipped him. She was so absorbed in his heroism that she had no thought even for his dampness. As Carl's eyes met hers she seemed to him to grow younger. And there came into his mind all the rumour that had vaguely reached him coupling their names together; and also his early dreams of love and passion and a marriage that would be one long honeymoon. And he saw how absurd had been those early dreams. He saw that the best chance of a felicitous marriage lay in a union of mature and serious persons, animated by grave interests and lofty ideals. Yes, she was older than he. But not much, not much! Not more than – how many years? And he remembered surprising her rapt glance that very evening as she watched him playing the piano. What had romance to do with age? Romance could occur at any age. It was occurring now. Her soft eyes, her portly form, exuded romance. And had not the renowned Beaconsfield espoused a lady appreciably older than himself, and did not those espousals achieve the ideal of bliss? In the act of saving the cat he had not been definitely aware that it was so particularly the cat of the household. But now, influenced by her attitude and her shining reverence, he actually did begin to persuade himself that an uncontrollable instinctive desire to please her and win her for his own had moved him to undertake the perilous passage of the sloping roof.

In short, the idle chatter of the town was about to be justified. In another moment he might have dripped into her generous arms . . . had not Miss Ebag swept into the drawing-room!

'Gracious!' gasped Miss Ebag. 'The poor dear thing will have pneumonia. Sister, you know his chest is not strong. Dear Mr Ullman, please, please, do go and – er – change.'

He did the discreet thing and went to bed, hot whisky following him on a tray carried by the housemaid.

VI

The next morning the slightly unusual happened. It was the custom for Carl Ullman to breakfast alone, while reading the *Staffordshire Signal*. The ladies Ebag breakfasted mysteriously in bed. But on this morning Carl found Miss Ebag before him in the breakfast-room. She prosecuted minute inquiries as to his health and nerves. She went out with him to regard the rhododendron bushes, and shuddered at the sight of the ruin which had saved him. She said, following famous philosophers, that Chance was merely the name we give to the effect of laws which we cannot understand. And, upon this high level of conversation, she poured forth his coffee and passed his toast.

It was a lovely morning after the tempest.

Goldie, all newly combed, and looking as though he had never seen a roof, strolled pompously into the room with tail unfurled. Miss Ebag picked the animal up and kissed it passionately.

'Darling!' she murmured, not exactly to Mr Ullman, nor yet exactly to the cat. Then she glanced effulgently at Carl and said, 'When I think that you risked your precious life, in that awful storm, to save my poor Goldie? . . . You must have guessed how dear he was to me? . . . No, really, Mr Ullman, I cannot thank you properly! I can't express my –'

Her eyes were moist.

Although not young, she was two years younger. Her age was two years less. The touch of man had never profaned her. No masculine kiss had ever rested on that cheek, that mouth. And Carl felt that he might be the first to cull the flower that had so long waited. He did not see, just then, the hollow beneath her chin, the two lines of sinew that, bounding a depression, disappeared beneath her collarette. He saw only her soul. He guessed that she would be more malleable than the widow, and he was sure that she was not in a position, as the widow was, to make comparisons between husbands. Certainly there appeared to be some confusion as to the proprietorship of this cat. Certainly he could not have saved the cat's life for love of two different persons. But that was beside the point. The essential thing was that he began to be glad that he had decided nothing definite about the widow on the previous evening.

'Darling!' said she again, with a new access of passion, kissing Goldie, but darting a glance at Carl.

He might have put to her the momentous question, between two bites of buttered toast, had not Mrs Ebag, at the precise instant, swum amply into the room.

'Sister! You up!' exclaimed Miss Ebag.

'And you, Sister!' retorted Mrs Ebag.

VII

It is impossible to divine what might have occurred for the delectation of the very ancient borough of Oldcastle if that frivolous piece of goods, Edith, had not taken it into her head to run down from London for a few days, on the plea that London was too ridiculously hot. She was a pretty girl, with fluffy honey-coloured hair and about thirty white frocks. And she seemed to be quite as silly as her staid stepmother and her prim step-aunt had said. She transformed the careful order of the house into a wild disorder, and left a novel or so lying on the drawing-room table between her stepmother's *Contemporary Review* and her step-aunt's *History of European Morals*. Her taste in music was candidly and brazenly bad. It was a fact, as her elders had stated, that she played nothing but waltzes. What was worse, she compelled Carl Ullman to perform waltzes. And one day she burst into the drawing-room when Carl was alone there, with a roll under her luscious arm, and said:

'What do you think I've found at Barrowfoot's?'

'I don't know,' said Carl, gloomily smiling, and then smiling without gloom.

'Waldteufel's waltzes arranged for four hands. You must play them with me at once.'

And he did. It was a sad spectacle to see the organist of St Placid's galloping through a series of dances with the empty-headed Edith.

The worst was, he liked it. He knew that he ought to prefer the high intellectual plane, the severe artistic tastes, of the elderly sisters. But he did not. He was amazed to discover that frivolity appealed more powerfully to his secret soul. He was also amazed to discover that his gloom was leaving him. This vanishing of gloom gave him strange sensations, akin to the sensations of a man who, after having worn gaiters into middle-age, abandons them.

After the Waldteufel she began to tell him all about herself; how she went slumming in the East End, and how jolly it was. And how she helped in the Bloomsbury Settlement, and how jolly that was. And, later, she said:

'You must have thought it very odd of me, Mr Ullman, not thanking you for so bravely rescuing my poor cat; but the truth is I never heard of it till today. I can't say how grateful I am. I should have loved to see you doing it.'

'Is Goldie your cat?' he feebly inquired.

'Why, of course,' she said. 'Didn't you know? Of course

you did! Goldie always belonged to me. Grandpa bought him for me. But I couldn't do with him in London, so I always leave him here for them to take care of. He adores me. He never forgets me. He'll come to me before anyone. You must have noticed that. I can't say how grateful I am! It was perfectly marvellous of you! I can't help laughing, though, whenever I think what a state mother and auntie must have been in that night!'

Strictly speaking, they hadn't a cent between them, except his hundred a year. But he married her hair and she married his melancholy eyes; and she was content to settle in Oldcastle, where there are almost no slums. And her stepmother was forced by Edith to make the hundred up to four hundred. This was rather hard on Mrs Ebag. Thus it fell out that Mrs Ebag remained a widow, and that Miss Ebag continues a flower unculled. However, gossip was stifled.

In his appointed time, and in the fulness of years, Goldie died, and was mourned. And by none was he more sincerely mourned than by the aged, bedridden Caiaphas.

'I miss my cat, I can tell ye!' said old Caiaphas pettishly to Carl, who was sitting by his couch. 'He knew his master, Goldie did! Edith did her best to steal him from me when you married and set up house. A nice thing considering I bought him and he never belonged to anybody but me! Ay! I shall never have another cat like that cat.'

And this is the whole truth of the affair.

The Steeple Cat *

J. V. von Scheffel

Here I sit, with clearest vision
   Gazing on the world and life,
Gazing from my proud position
   On that scene of party strife.

Smiling from the tower or steeple,
   Lo, the Cat all scornful stares
At the foolish pigmy people,
   Busied with their trifling cares.

Vain my thoughts – I cannot give them
   Access to my point of sight;
To their ignorance I leave them –
   Verily my loss is slight!

* The German poet and novelist Joseph Viktor von Scheffel (1826–86) is best known for his famous historical romance *Ekkehard* (set in a tenth-century monastery) and the immensely popular narrative poem *The Trumpeter of Säckingen* featuring the tomcat Hiddigeigei. This poem (untitled in the original) is one of the cat's thirteen songs.

Warped and poor the human spirit,
  Human deeds of small behoof:
Calm, in consciousness of merit,
  Sits the Cat upon the roof.

The Case of the Cross-eyed Sphinx and the Holy Ghost

Christopher Park

I'd decided to give up driving for Lent. This, of course, meant that any activities that required exercise in the motoring department would have to be carried out by my beloved wife Bunty, not necessarily a prospect I relished but perhaps a necessary evil if one is to hold to one's religious precepts, as I have been brought up to do. Not that I am a religious fanatic, mind you – after all, I felt I had to turn down the honour of becoming godfather to my old schoolpal Plugger Bastable's sprog recently when it became evident that I would have to stand up in front of a crowd of people in church and swear that I would abjure the Devil and believed that everything in the Bible was gospel and all that. It seemed a bit steep, I thought, especially as Plugger and his missus (now divorced, I should add) hadn't been to church since her father died three years ago. No, I'm a 'traditional' believer, as it were. Part of the British way of life and all that – just so long as it doesn't involve me having to lie in public, that's all.

Bunty, of course, is rather the other way. This is primarily because her father, Septimus Heythrop Scroope – formerly the 13th Baron Heythrop of Markwych – had been a padre in the RAF. So she'd had a lot more religion in her background from Day One. The trouble is, as with all the Scroopes, that she'd also had an overdose of cat worship from about the same period. This I was becoming aware of by degrees as we visited her various in-laws periodically. Her father had been one of twelve children, and since our marriage last November we had been gradually working our way through the relatives. This month, as Mother's Day fell on a convenient weekend, it would be the turn of Mater and Pater Scroope themselves at the family home near Stratford.

The only problem, though, was transport. Having given up driving for the duration, I had managed to make do locally by trotting down to the post office and the like on the Major, our chestnut. Though a mare and deserving perhaps of a more feminine name, Bunty had insisted, and so it stuck. On reflection, I suppose, it is no more daft than calling a totally asexual machine by a woman's name, as sailors do their ships in nearby Portsmouth. And indeed the reason I have been riding the Major at all frequently of late is because of my Lenten scruples apropos conducting my beautiful 1936 Lagonda, Hermione, on to the thoroughfare. Now the thought of cantering up the M1 to Stratford on the Major had crossed my mind, but Bunty would have none of it, not even when I suggested we hitched up both horses to a buggy owned by one of our neighbours in Liss.

The upshot of it all was that we had a number of alternatives – to let Bunty drive Hermione, to go in her little tin VW Golf, to hire a car or to take public transport – all of which seemed less than inviting. There was, however, one additional possibility, which was to cadge a lift. And as it was Mother's Day, there was every chance that B.'s sister Catherine would be going up from Southsea, together with her husband and two children, in her monstrous Mk IX Jaguar. A phone call revealed that this was indeed the case but that her spouse was currently working in Moscow, trying to set up a trade link. As a result, there would be more space in the car and she would welcome a hand controlling the brats while she was driving. And so it was arranged – Catherine would pick us up *en route*, as we were only just off the A3, directly north of her house.

When the *Jour de Maman* arrived we all piled into the Jag, B., late as ever as she said goodbye to Hickey, our estate manager, leaving a large lipstick kiss on his cheek. I couldn't really see that this was necessary, nor her helping him button up his open-necked shirt where there seemed to be a similar red mark on his neck – indeed, two or three – but I expect she just wanted to make sure he didn't catch cold and pass it on to the horses while we were away. Oh, what a treasure she is! So, shoving the twins further along the leather seat, I slid in and closed the back door. Bunty got into the front, Catherine slung it into first and the huge swept-back beast with a bonnet the size of a double-bed thundered off.

On the motorway, in between playing 'I Spy' and 'Snap' with cars (though we didn't see any Mk IX Jags and had to make do with later models), I managed to piece together a little more of the Scroope family history from B. and C. in preparation for our meeting with their parents who, perhaps surprisingly, I had yet to meet. They hadn't made it to our wedding, which had been a rather hurried affair with mostly Memburys present.

I also filled Catherine in a bit more on my own background, explaining that my elder brother had inherited the bulk of my father's estate on his death just before our marriage, when he surprised us all by returning from

Burma. Otherwise I would now be master of Membury Manor and its vast acres rather than the Place, which was effectively its bothy. C. was a bit churlish in this regard, I thought, as I was explaining, and gave Bunty a look which my wife countered with a comment to the effect that she loved me anyway, even if I wasn't rich. Warmed by this, I took her hand and added that we did at least have a small estate with a trout farm and a few sheep and chickens to live off, and of course we had each other. In the ensuing silence in which even the children seem to expect B. to add something, she suddenly shouted, 'Snap!' and everyone looked out the windows, but no Jaguars were visible.

By the time we arrived at the gates of a large thatched villa not far from Anne Hathaway's cottage on the outskirts of Stratford I had learnt some fascinating but rather uncomfortable truths about Bunty's and Catherine's side of the Scroope family that had been somewhat glossed over in the first months of our married life. For reasons best known to himself – though I gather these included the war, politics, his social conscience, seeing the Light, whatever – as a young man her father had sold the ancestral pile, given away a fortune, publicly dropped his title and, after his maiden speech, never again sat in the House of Lords. Instead he had studied for the Church, become a fervent member of the cloth and, when hostilities broke out, volunteered to serve as an RAF padre. When Bunty and Catherine grew up, however, they kept the honorific 'Honourable', as they were perfectly entitled to do as children of a peer. They were also, it transpired, doubly Scroopes, as not only was their father born one but their mother was too . . . Dr Septimus Heythrop Scroope was their mother's uncle! This naturally had caused consternation in the family, especially as, at the time of her first pregnancy, Bunty's mother had been only fifteen and Septimus was twenty years older.

An intelligent, pretty and sexually inquisitive child with a woman's body in every imaginable respect, she had taken to dressing the part and the RAF chaplain, visiting long-forgotten relations on leave, had been entranced and sufficiently confused by the girl's adult looks and behaviour to take the ultimate liberty. Not that she had minded too much, of course, as the birth in quick succession of Bunty's younger sister Catherine and younger brother Bryan bore witness. But it had led to Septimus being defrocked.

It had perhaps also contributed to the gradual unhingeing of her mother's mind. Madeleine Scroope – Maddy for short, or Mad to the unkind – had latterly turned completely bonkers. The first signs had been discernible even at the birth of their children and was further evidenced by their names. My wife's real name, it turned out, was not Arabinta shortened to Bunty, as she later gave out, but rather Brunty, the real surname of the Brontë sisters' father, who changed it to the more familiar one in honour of Lord Nelson's title, Duke of Brontë. A similar contrivance hid her brother Bryan's actual names, Branwell Heathcliff, reflecting a further obsession with the family from Hawarth Parsonage. But the unkindest hand of all was dealt to Catherine, who had been legally christened Currer Acton Ellis Scroope. We were to discover further examples of Maddy's insanity over the weekend . . .

Mrs Scroope herself came out to meet us at the door when the giant motor crunched to a halt on the driveway. In her hand she carried a camcorder and everything possible was caught by it: the children running out to greet her, the kiss from her two daughters, even my outstretched hand after I had managed to put one of the two heavy cases under my left arm. In an attempt to grab her free left hand with my right and peck her on the cheek I only succeeded in bruising my eye on the camera lens.

We were then shown in – or rather ushered before the camera – and eventually settled down in the comfortable lounge with its open-hearth fire, upright piano and standard lamps. Conversation at first, however, was rather difficult as Maddy continued to film from a seated position and swung the machine at each of us in turn as we spoke. This was most uncanny – a bit like talking to a Dalek – and was further aggravated when she found herself shooting into the light of a window behind me and asked me to move elsewhere, so my face wouldn't be in the shade, and to repeat everything I had just said.

All this was starting to irritate me, and the others too, when a handsome man of about my age entered from the staircase adjoining the lounge, beckoned to a burly-looking fellow in a white shirt and waistcoat to take the cases to our rooms, and joined us. This, it turned out, was the brother Bryan, aka Branwell.

'Now, come on, Mother,' he began, taking away the camera from Maddy's clawlike hands. 'Everyone's come to see you, not your video-recorder, and I expect they find it difficult to talk as if they're acting when all they want to do is talk. Now, why don't you open your presents and tell them about your latest book?'

He indicated the pile of gaily wrapped parcels we'd deposited on the table as we'd arrived, and I retrieved a potted chrysanthemum from a carrier-bag I'd left in the hall as she sat down.

The delight was evident on the old lady's face as she began to tear open the paper, ably assisted by the two five-year-olds, whose eyes shone with excitement. One thing I hadn't expected, though, was the second manifestation of my mother-in-law's mental instability –

her storytelling. All the while as she opened the presents – soap, toiletries, chocolates, pot-pourri and so forth – she recited, or rather incanted, it seemed to me, the narrative of some imaginary Gothic novel. I say 'imaginary' to dispel any thought that, had it been written down, it would actually have constituted a book for the simple reason that it never really got anywhere. Sentence after sentence began, first with one character and then with another, but never reached a conclusion. Except, that is, when she barked . . . After for or five attempts to complete a sentence, like a child's clockwork toy bumping up against a wall she would make a sudden honking sound – she was literally barking mad.

The children found their grandmother's mannerisms hilarious at first but then became tearful as she continued to recite in a monotone. This confused the old lady even more; she wasn't entirely aware of her actions. Thus at the same time as she smiled on the twins and wanted to fondle them in a natural, grandmotherly way, she would continue with her ever faster monotonous mutterings, then emit a sudden bark like a hiccup, which made them run from her lap. After half an hour or so of this, Bryan/Branwell produced a matchbox, out of which projected a tiny crank-handle, and gave it to her. This proved to be a miniature musical box which played the 'William Tell Overture' and absorbed Mrs Scroope – who cranked the handle at various speeds – for some time while we adjourned to our rooms upstairs prior to a late lunch.

When the gong sounded and we descended again, we encountered the missing link in my wife's immediate family: her father Septimus. He was a large, bluff-looking man, not entirely unlike the elder G. K. Chesterton, with his corpulent figure and mass of silver-grey hair, but with one exception – he had no legs.

'You'll forgive me if I don't get up,' he said cheerily from his wheelchair as we gathered around the dining-table and shook hands. 'Septimus Scroope. And I presume you are Tobias of the noble Membury clan. Had some contact with your father out in Burma during the war, you know.'

I was intrigued and said that in truth I knew little of that side of the family business as my elder brother looked after it all. Knowing that he'd been in the RAF, albeit as a padre, I politely alluded to his disability as perhaps an unfortunate sacrifice in the course of defending King and Country.

'Not a bit of it, old man. Damned stupid shooting accident a couple of years ago – blew me blessed foot off. Damned stupid as I only had one at the time anyway, having lost the other from smoking – hardened arteries and all that. Pretty damned stupid.'

I smiled sheepishly but was also impressed that a one-legged man could even think of going shooting in the first place: the problem of balance with the recoil of a twelve-bore shotgun would be considerable. Not that I knew much about it, of course, never having indulged. I revealed my thoughts to him.

'Never been shooting, eh? Tell you what. We can go and blast some clays later if you like.'

'That would be marvellous,' I replied. 'That is, so long as Mrs Scroope has no objections. It is Mother's Day, of course.'

I looked at Bunty and her mother, who had sat down on the far side of the large oval table heaped with turkey, vegetables and all manner of cutlery and glassware.

'What's that? "Jenny entered the darkened room . . . Matilda heard a scream in the attic . . . From the top of the castle walls Marcus could see a shadowy . . ." BARK! Going out shooting? No, my dear. Yes, cabbage only, please, and just one potato. "Down, down she fell . . . Marcus saw her

124

dress spread out in the air . . . The drawbridge was up, was up, was up . . ." BARK!'

I sat down and took the vegetables proffered by my wife. The food was delicious, but the meal was, to say the least, rather trying. When Mrs Scroope began reciting at the top of her voice, Bryan left the table and retrieved her camera. This stopped the noise but I then had the unpleasant experience of her filming every mouthful I took, kneeling down beside my chair with the camera pointed up at forty-five degrees to my face. This was not a happy experience, as can be imagined, and I was glad when the pudding was finished and Septimus and I were able to slip out of the back door and leave the womenfolk with Bryan and the children. The adults, after all, had got used to their mother over a number of years, and the children would treat it all as a bit of fun. To me it was all rather a strain.

The garden was very pleasant as I strolled behind my father-in-law's electric wheechair, and I was admiring the lime grove either side of the path we were following when he suddenly shot ahead at great speed. Stunned, I raced after him, thinking that the machine had somehow got out of control but, try as I might, I couldn't catch him. He flashed around the side of a large, apparently triangular, concrete blockhouse which marked the end of the path, and from both sides of which fanned out a fence of poplars, presumably marking the end of the garden.

A few minutes later I reached the blockhouse, which must, I suppose, have been at least three hundred yards from the thatched homestead we'd left. I was working my way round to the right in the direction Septimus had gone when I heard the sound of a lawn-mower engine and, emerging, as it were, at the base of the triangle, was just in time to witness my father-in-law flying through the air.

Lest it be thought that I too was beginning to suffer from the family madness, I should explain that what in fact I saw was Septimus Scroope in his high-powered wheelchair, to the back of which had been strapped what to all intents and purposes was a microlight aircraft. The rear of the building, I could now see, abutted on to a long runway which from the air must have looked like a large arrow, with the triangular blockhouse at its head.

As he now circled and swooped in the spring sunlight, I could make out that he was holding something in his hand. A few minutes later, as he skimmed the neighbouring fields, it became evident from two loud reports that this was a double-barrelled shotgun. The noise was followed by a salvo of imprecations, culminating in a loud 'Damn' as the machine curved back and began to descend towards the runway in my direction.

Flabbergasted by this display, I walked up to where my father-in-law had touched down and applauded as he switched off the engine, unharnessed the flying attachment – which slid away on wheels – and drove his wheelchair towards me.

'Bravo.' I clapped. 'That was amazing. But what were you shooting at?'

'Sorry about that, old man. Got rather carried away. Most impolite. Had this trouble with a fox. Keep rabbits, you see.' He pointed to a hutch near the building. 'Damned nuisance. Saw the bounder as we were walking up the path – think I winged him, though. Damn and blast! I'll get him next time. But come in, come into my abode, indeed my sanctuary.'

The concrete blockhouse, which had given no evidence of glass on its two approaching sides, now revealed a large, sliding picture window in the centre of its base, and it was through this that we entered. It led into a sort of airlock porch where umbrellas, overcoats, the gun-rack – into which he leant the shotgun he was carrying – and a sort of giant Ali Baba basket were stored to either side, and then, passing over some coconut matting, we went through another sliding window. I remarked on the miraculous automatic opening mechanism.

'Oh, that,' said Septimus. 'It's a simple pressure-plate device I installed. It's a great help with the wheelchair. You open it by rolling on the mat outside and close it by rolling on the one inside. Going from inside out has the same effect. The only problem is remembering to switch it off by remote control on the way out, otherwise all and sundry would be trolling in.'

As we entered, we were greeted by a stretching black cat which had evidently been awakened by the sound of the aircraft and the gunshots. But this was no ordinary cat. Not only did it have no whiskers – it had no hair either. I was dumbfounded until Septimus explained.

'I see you've not met one of these before, my boy. This little chap is what is known as a Sphinx or Hairless cat. Apart from its lack of whiskers, its golden eyes and large ears, its most striking feature is the strange, apparently hairless coat. The breed is a modern recreation of the original Mexican Hairless cat which died out in the early 1900s. Apparently they were Aztec cats and were very intelligent, with a sort of mousey skin. This little chap, Moriarty his name is, is not quite so bright and, as you can see, somewhat cross-eyed. He's actually Maddy's, as I'm not awfully keen on cats, but he gets so distraught every time the old girl barks that it seemed unkind to keep him in the house.'

At the name Moriarty I perked up and told Septimus that since my marriage I had been engrossed in the writings of the Blessed Conan Doyle and had read and reread all the Sherlock Holmes stories till I knew them by heart. As a result, I felt as well educated in the arts of detection as anyone could be. I went to stroke Moriarty as I spoke and received in return a scratched hand and a loud hiss.

'Ah. Sorry about that,' Septimus said. 'We decided on Moriarty, the name of Holmes's evil opponent, for good reason, you see. Basically he is the most cussed cat ever known. But can he use his temper to catch something and prove his worth? Nothing doing. I don't know if it has something to do with his crossed eyes, but he seems incapable of playing with a ball, let alone a rat. Which brings me to our other resident pest – a white mouse, which I have christened the Holy Ghost because he seems to be everywhere. Moriarty has been trying to catch him for nearly three years now, but to no avail. Every time he slips away. In fact, I have a theory that this is all about yin and yang. The cat and the mouse complement each other like the sun and the moon; if ever one catches the other our world will end. So big black Moriarty, representing the forces of Evil, is constantly on the trail of the tiny white Holy Ghost, representing the forces of Good. It is a fine balance, rather like the two opposing Conan Doyle characters. Did you know that "Sherlock" means "white-haired?"'

I confessed that I didn't. I was greatly impressed by all this and was equally interested in his views on religion, seen from the perspective of a defrocked priest. I asked him to expand on the topic.

'Well,' he began, as we moved further into the triangular open-plan bungalow and he waved me on to a bean-bag seat, 'let's approach this from a different angle. Let us, in fact, start off with angles. "Not Angles but angels," as St Augustine said when discussing the native tribes of Britain. Look around you.' He indicated the room with its single bed, kitchenette, sitar and wooden African masks. 'I built this from concrete blocks sold for assembling kit-garages with so that I could have somewhere to live near Maddy. Though we were never married – the Church wouldn't allow an uncle to marry his niece – we used to live together as man and wife, but since her, er . . . troubles, it hasn't been easy. So what shape do I choose for the building? A triangle: the Holy Trinity. And because I love aircraft I had my little runway constructed so that from the air the building looks like an arrowhead and, with the fringe of poplars running either side of it, the walls resemble a propeller. And the whole caboodle points directly at Coventry airport's runway, which ensures that lot of planes overfly the estate, using it as an orientation aid.'

'But one thing strikes me,' I interrupted. 'If you are so keen on aircraft, why is there so little evidence of this in your home?'

'Ah,' he said, 'that is deliberate. I do not have any aero memorabilia or pictures in the house to prevent myself from filling it up with them. Even the fuel for the microlight is heavily disguised. Can you guess where it is? In the Ali Baba basket in the porch. In fact, the furnishings you see around you are all objects I detest. The whole point is to try to create a constant tension, which I escape from by flying. If everything on this earth was as we wanted it, we would be happy here and would do nothing. We would simply ossify. Come over here.'

He trundled across the floor to an area at the back of the room which was raised higher than the rest. Locked into a lift mechanism, his wheelchair slid up the side of a staircase which I mounted on foot. At the top the platform contained a desk, an Anglepoise, bookshelves and, near the lift, a long row of overlapping pieces of paper.

'This' – he indicated the line of papers on the floor –

'is my memory system. By nature I am an immensely tidy person, but I have a weak memory. So, as an aide-memoire, I make a mess on the floor. Each of these piles is something I have to do today. I hate having them on the floor, but if they weren't there, I would forget what I have to do. And, as I never get everything done each day anyway, the tension is maintained. It's a vicious circle. But there are ways out. The simplest is to run away – ignore it, escape, go on holiday, fly a plane, drive an expensive car . . .'

Suddenly my thoughts returned to Hermione and what I had given up for Lent and why. 'But how does that solve anything?' I asked.

'It doesn't. You're quite right,' he replied. 'When you return, everything is as it was before. So what's a second option? Well, to destroy it, of course. Cut the Gordian knot, blow it all away, kill the fox, become a murderer. That's where I find the guns so useful – destruction brings with it strange pleasures. But rubbing out a problem doesn't solve it, any more than wiping an unfinished equation off the blackboard gives you the answer.'

'So what is the answer?' I asked, transformed into a young student at the feet of his guru.

'Why, creation, of course. The building, as it were, of complementary systems in the hope that these will eventually produce a happier result. In the same way as inoculation introduces into the body a mild form of a disease to build up our immunity. As the Bible says: "Go forth and multiply."'

'I think I see,' I said, finding that by not trying to stroke the cat it had curled up in my lap of its own accord. 'So you could, for example, replace your memory system by, say, a list of things to do, or you could employ a secretary.'

'Well, almost. My memory system is related to my current work. Probably the happiest solution to the problems that surround it would be to do some completely different kind of work altogether – more important work, which would make the whole of the old business redundant . . .'

We had continued in this manner for some hours when a light flashing by the sliding windows indicated to us that supper was about to be served, and we locked Moriarty in and returned to the main house.

It struck me as rather unfair to lock the cat inside with all those fields around, but Septimus assured me it was for the best, as the local animals would probably kill the strange-looking cat.

'I can't understand why they decided to call it a Sphinx cat,' I said. 'Is there something inscrutable about it? I mean, I thought the sphinx whose puzzle Oedipus solved was supposed to be a sort of winged chimera and not particularly feline.'

'No,' replied Septimus. 'You're thinking of the Greek sphinx. The Egyptian one had the head of a woman and the body of a lion, which is rather more cat-like and probably accounts for the breed's name. Though Moriarty certainly has a very unfeminine face.'

We laughed and I recalled from my schooldays the riddle Oedipus had solved: 'What walks on four legs in the morning, two legs at midday and three legs in the evening?' Sadly the riddle would have to be reworked for Septimus, for the answer, 'Man' (the third leg is a walking stick in old age), no longer applied to him. It would have to be 'four wheels in the evening', which didn't have quite the same ring to it.

I shared my ruminations with my father-in-law and we laughed again. He seemed a jolly sort of fellow despite the setbacks in his life, and I began to warm to him considerably. Out of respect, as we walked I battled again with the philosophy he'd outlined.

'Now if I've understood what you've said correctly, Septimus, how about if you locked up Moriarty in a cage so that he couldn't possibly catch the Holy Ghost? Wouldn't that solve the problem and prevent Evil from ever conquering Good?'

'Nice try, son, but that would be no different from locking up the mouse or shooting both of them. It would break the natural order. Sure, it happens in the real world – think of all the little old ladies who are locked up in their houses for fear of hoodlums who, instead of being imprisoned themselves, roam and terrorise at will. But it's just a blocking move, an interference in the natural order. And as a seventh son of a seventh son – hence my name, as I'm sure you realised – I am a great believer in the order of things.

'No, another solution that I didn't mention is the involvement of some outside agency by accident. This coincidental alteration of the situation, the moving of the goal posts, in effect, would also bring release from the cycle. This is God or Hope, but not 'hope' in the conventional active sense. If you actively try to make a coincidence happen, it never does. Meanwhile, though, you must strive to create and find the solution yourself – after all, life is too short to sit waiting for an accident that may never take place. It's a bit like the old saying: "The Lord helps those who help themselves . . ."'

By now my brain was getting into hopeless knots of its own devising, but luckily we had reached the house and entered.

Supper was a re-enactment of the crazy round of entertainment we had had at lunch: Maddy either filming or reciting, the twins screaming at each other and Bunty and her sister talking nineteen to the dozen while Bryan looked on impassively.

Happily, it was a somewhat briefer affair and we were soon able to leave the table. At this point Maddy decided to run back through the day's video-tape and watch our activities on the TV monitor. For the rest of us this proved almost more boring than actually being filmed. After the first few minutes of interest as we checked how our clothing – and in the women's case, make-up – looked on screen, we soon tired of it. Not so Maddy, who sat entranced, all the while incanting her stories.

It was then that I had my first idea, which seemed to me to put into practice some of Septimus's principles. What if someone were to take a video of *her*, muttering away in her nonsensical way, and then to play it back to her on the screen? I discussed this with Septimus, who thought it a splendid proposal and certainly worth a try. This made me feel very proud, and I could even see Bunty's eyes shining in admiration. All agreed that, as I had thought of it, I should be the cameraman.

After filming her from every angle for about ten minutes as she watched her family at lunch on the TV – including the scene where she pointed the lens practically up my nose during the soup course – I rewound the camcorder and took out the film for Catherine to place in the playback machine. This resulted in an immediate spate of protest barking from Maddy, but by craftily putting the old tape behind her back and swapping it for the new, Catherine led her mother to believe that the old one had been reinstated. The first few minutes were a continuation of dinner (she'd had to change tapes during the meal), but then the film cut to her, seated in front of the TV, chanting and barking – the picture zooming in and out as I had intended it to when adjusting the lens.

The effect on Maddy was stunning. She simply stopped

133

talking, watched for a few minutes, then announced in a perfectly calm voice that she was going upstairs.

Everyone was amazed, and I was heartily congratulated by the whole company. Bryan followed Maddy to her room, where she apparently got into bed and went to sleep.

My in-laws' happiness knew no bounds. The children were packed off to bed as well – it now being after nine and quite dark outside – and the rest of us settled down in the front room.

About twenty minutes later, when a breeze began to rattle the windows, Septimus remembered that he had promised to take me shooting and had also left the microlight unsecured on the runway.

'Could I ask you a big favour, Tobias?' he said. 'I am a bit nervous about the wind picking up again and smashing the little plane – would you nip back to my house and push it into the porch? You can pick up the shotguns at the same time and we can bag a few clays first thing in the morning. Now that Maddy seems a little better, I think I'll stay the night here. And going out in the cold won't do my chest any good.'

'Of course,' I replied and, taking the remote-control door opener he proffered, started walking towards the door.

'Why not take the Old Trundler?' he suggested.

Mystified, I allowed him to overtake me and followed him to a shed at the left of the back door. In it I found what appeared to be a converted go-cart. It was a petrol-driven tricycle-wheelchair and was kept as a spare in case the batteries of Septimus's main charger ever ran down. I was more than pleased, as it would be a long walk there and back on a cold night otherwise.

'The only problem,' Septimus warned, 'is that it hasn't got any lights. You'll have to take a torch.'

The one he gave me seemed to flicker a lot, so I asked for a candle and some matches as well, just in case.

A couple of tugs at the starter rope got the engine going, and in a few minutes I was buzzing down the pathway towards my father-in-law's house, waving the torch in front of me with one hand and trying to steer with the other.

The wind had indeed picked up, and by the time I reached the aircraft it had tipped on to its side and its wings were being put under considerable pressure. It was at this point that the torch went dead. It was now pitch-black. I had opted to keep the motor running on the go-cart in case it stopped for good and I had to walk back in the dark. It was a sound idea, but unfortunately the machine was one step ahead of me. The engine sputtered, then fell silent. I lit the candle and checked the petrol tank – it was empty.

Moving over to the microlight, I could see that though there was some fuel left inside, the structure was too cumbersome to allow me to transfer it from one machine to the other. So it was going to be a walk back after all.

The main task, however, was to get the aircraft inside the porch, and to this end I carefully approached the door with my remote locking/unlocking device. A gust of wind caught the candle and blew it out, but not before I had managed to engage the release mechanism.

The window opened. Not knowing where the light switches were, I lit the candle again and leant it against one of the guns, being careful to keep it away from the nearby box of cartridges. The window closed behind me, preventing the flame from being blown out.

I stood on the mat again and passed through the window, which once more closed behind me, and headed for the aircraft. I righted it and pushed it towards the glass doors; they parted and I shoved the structure in. It was when I stood back to lock the window that I realised the doorway was now completely blocked and, try as I might, I could no longer reach the candle. Moreover, as the leading edge of the wings was curved and the trailing edge flat, I could no longer pull the plane out again.

By now exhausted, I felt that I could do no better than go back to the house and enlist some help. I reasoned that Septimus must have forgotten to tell me how to fold down the wings but that it didn't matter too much: the candle would be safe enough for a few minutes and nobody would be able to break in, as the doorway was completely blocked. And so I began the long walk back in search of help – or, at least, further instructions.

I had just opened the back door when a small black shape flashed past me. Bemused, I followed it to the front room where the others were playing whist.

'Well, I'm blessed,' Septimus said. 'Take a look at this, Tobias.' He held up Moriarty, in whose mouth were the fast-expiring remains of a white mouse.

'Good grief,' I exclaimed. 'The Sphinx has caught the Holy Ghost – the cycle has been broken. What can this mean?'

'What it means, my dear fellow,' Septimus replied, 'is that you let the damned cat out of my house. But no matter. Once it's out, it's out.' He extracted the poor mouse from the cat's jaws, and Moriarty immediately slipped away and out of the back door. 'Any joy with the guns and the plane?' Septimus asked.

Reluctantly I admitted that I had failed to finish the job, explained the difficulty and asked if Bryan would come and help. Bunty's brother was more than happy to oblige and, after he had put on his overcoat and galoshes, we set off up the path together.

We'd taken hardly more than a few paces when the sky suddenly lit up and there was an enormous explosion. We ran forward as fast as we could, but it was no use. By the time we reached the triangular building, my father-in-law's home was a ball of flame.

A few days after Bunty and I had returned to Liss, I got a letter from Septimus Scroope. It ran as follows:

Dear Tobias,

It was good to meet you last weekend and, though I am naturally rather saddened by all that occurred, I realise that it wasn't entirely your fault. Indeed, it may well be that considerable good will come about as a result of the catastrophic damage that resulted from your visit.

As I say, to be fair, you weren't completely to blame. I should have told you where the light switches were in the house; I should have explained how to fold the wings of the plane together like a wheechair or baby's pushchair. You weren't to know. But a naked light is a dangerous thing in a house full of wooden artefacts and lots of paperwork – especially if it is left in the vicinity of shotgun cartridges and a large tank of petrol hidden in an Ali Baba basket . . .

However, even the candle might have been safe enough if it hadn't been for two factors you omitted to take note of, and which I am sure your Blessed Conan Doyle would have pointed out to you. These were the cat and the pressure mat.

After presenting me with the Holy Ghost, Moriarty must have headed straight back to the warmth of the

Trinity at full speed, not realising there was no way back in. But then the cat sat on the mat, as it were, and 'Open, Sesame!' – in the words of Ali Baba and the forty thieves in the story – the doors parted because you had omitted to lock the mechanism in your haste. The cat, discovering his way blocked by the microlight, headed for the only space visible – beside the candle. In the process, unfortunately, he must have knocked it over, setting fire to the coconut matting and *bingo!* (or rather *bango!*), the cartridges, the fuel and the aircraft's petrol tank blasted the place apart.

Moriarty, I am pleased to say, survived, though a little shaken. The explosion cleared the aircraft from the doorway and, reflected by the concrete wedge shape behind, literally blew the cat clean out on to the runway. The walls later collapsed in a heap and no longer resemble an arrowhead from the air; the rows of poplars were also burnt to the ground, thereby destroying the propeller effect.

Well, so much for the negative side.

On the positive, there were, surprisingly perhaps, some good results. My wife Maddy, though very shaken by the explosion and the effect your video had on her, no longer mutters crazy stories to herself or films everybody. Also partly because of this and partly because you destroyed my home I have moved back into the main house, together with the cat. Moriarty has also contributed to my wife's improvement and, now that she has stopped barking, is happy to be petted by her once again.

From the philosophical point of view, your actions have, if anything, had an even more dramatic effect on my life.

You destroyed my aircraft, my only joy and release from this earthly cycle of pain.

You also blew up the rabbit hutch, thus allowing the creatures to escape into the wild and thereby releasing me from the aggravation of constant raids by foxes and my urge to shoot Old Reynard from my plane.

You destroyed not only my memory system but also the research from which it all stemmed.

And, finally, you destroyed the hateful furnishings of a man who likes planes. I now have a photograph of my old Hurricane on my study wall and spend most of my time gardening, with my wife and my cat by my side.

I am a happy man, Thank you.

PS. Though you may be tempted to think that an external agency, the hand of God, etc., was instrumental in changing my life – exactly along the lines I outlined to you when you arrived last weekend – please, please, forget it. Nearer the truth may be the fact that when the words of a fool combine with the actions of an idiot, any survivors can count themselves lucky . . .

Love Letters of Clerical Cats *

Erasmus Darwin and Anna Seward

From the Persian Snow, at Dr Darwin's, to Miss Po Felina, at the Palace, Lichfield

Lichfield Vicarage
Sept. 7, 1780

Dear Miss Pussey,

As I sat, the other day, basking myself in the Dean's Walk, I saw you, in your stately palace, washing your beautiful round face, and elegantly brindled ears, with your velvet paws, and whisking about, with graceful sinuosity, your meandering tail. That treacherous hedgehog, Cupid, concealed himself behind your tabby beauties, and darting one of his too well aimed quills, pierced, O cruel imp! my fluttering heart.

---

* Dr Erasmus Darwin (1731–1802), grandfather of the naturalist Charles Darwin, brother of the rector of Elston and himself no stranger to religious controversy, was a physican, botanist, poet and hymn writer. He lived in the old vicarage in Lichfield, Staffordshire, and became very friendly with the poet Anna Seward, who lived with her father, Thomas Seward, prebendary of Lichfield, in the nearby Bishop's Palace. These letters by Darwin and Seward, supposedly written by their two cats, were published in Seward's biography of Darwin.

Ever since that fatal hour have I watched, day and night, in my balcony, hoping that the stillness of the starlight evenings might induce you to take the air on the leads of the palace. Many serenades have I sung under your windows; and, when you failed to appear, with the sound of my voice made the vicarage re-echo through all its winding lanes and dirty alleys. All heard me but my cruel Fair-one; she, wrapped in fur, sat purring with contented insensibility, or slept with untroubled dreams.

Though I cannot boast those delicate varieties of melody with which you sometimes ravish the ear of night, and stay the listening stars; though you sleep hourly on the lap of the favourite of the muses, and are patted by those fingers which hold the pen of science; and every day, with her permission, dip your white whiskers in delicious cream; yet am I not destitute of all advantages of birth, education, and beauty. Derived from Persian kings, my snowy fur yet retains the whiteness and splendour of their ermine.

This morning, as I sat upon the Doctor's tea-table, and saw my reflected features in the slop-basin, my long white whiskers, ivory teeth, and topaz eyes, I felt an agreeable presentiment of my suit; and certainly the slop-basin did not flatter me, which shews the azure flowers upon its borders less beauteous than they are.

You know not, dear Miss Pussey Po, the value of the address you neglect. New milk have I, in flowing abundance, and mice pent up in twenty garrets, for your food and amusement.

Permit me, this afternoon, to lay at your divine feet the head of an enormous Norway Rat, which has even now stained my paws with its gore. If you will do me the honour to sing the following song, which I have taken the liberty to write, as expressing the sentiments I wish you to entertain, I will bring a band of catgut and catcall, to accompany you in chorus.

(Air: *Spirituosi*)

Cats I scorn, who sleek and fat,
Shiver at a Norway Rat;
Rough and hardy, bold and free,
Be the cat that's made for me!
He, whose nervous paws can take
My lady's lapdog by the neck;
With furious hiss attack the hen,
And snatch a chicken from the pen.
If the treacherous swain should prove
Rebellious to my tender love,
My scorn the vengeful paw shall dart,
Shall tear his fur, and pierce his heart.

Chorus
Qu-ow wow, quall, wawl, moon.

Deign, most adorable charmer, to purr your assent to this my request, and believe me to be, with the profoundest respect, your true admirer,

Snow*

* The cat to whom the above letter was addressed had been broken of her propensity to kill birds, and lived several years without molesting a dove, a tame lark, and a red-breast, all of which used to fly about the room where the cat was daily admitted. The dove frequently sat on pussey's back, and the little birds would peck fearlessly from the plate in which she was eating.

Answer

I am but too sensible of the charms of Mr Snow; but while I admire the spotless whiteness of his ermine, and the tyger-strength of his commanding form, I sigh in secret, that he, who sucked the milk of benevolence and philosophy, should yet retain the extreme of that fierceness, too justly imputed to the Grimalkin race. Our hereditary violence is perhaps commendable when we exert it against the foes of our protectors, but deserves much blame when it annoys their friends.

The happiness of a refined education was mine; yet, dear Mr Snow, my advantages in that respect were not equal to what yours might have been; but, while you give unbounded indulgence to your carnivorous desires, I have so far subdued mine, that the lark pours his mattin song, the canarybird warbles wild and loud, and the robin pipes his farewell song to the setting sun, unmolested in my presence; nay, the plump and tempting dove has reposed securely upon my soft back, and bent her glossy neck in graceful curves as she walked around me.

But let me hasten to tell thee how my sensibilities in thy favour were, last month, unfortunately repressed. Once, in the noon of one of its most beautiful nights, I was invited abroad by the serenity of the amorous hour, secretly stimulated by the hope of meeting my admired Persian. With silent steps I paced around the dimly-gleaming leads of the palace. I had acquired a taste for scenic beauty and poetic imagery, by listening to ingenious observations upon their nature from the lips of thy own lord, as I lay purring at the feet of my mistress.

I admired the lovely scene, and breathed my sighs for thee to the listening moon. She threw the long shadows of the majestic cathedral upon the silvered lawn. I beheld the pearly meadows of Stow Valley, and the lake in its bosom, which, reflecting the lunar rays, seemed a sheet of diamonds. The trees of the Dean's Walk, which the hand of Dulness had been restrained from torturing into trim and detestable regularity, met each other in a thousand various and beautiful forms. Their liberated boughs danced on the midnight gale, and the edges of their leaves were whitened by the moonbeams. I descended to the lawn, that I might throw the beauties of the valley into perspective through the graceful arches, formed by their meeting branches. Suddenly my ear was startled, not by the voice of my lover, but by the loud and dissonant noise of the war-song, which six black Grimalkins were raising in honour of the numerous victories obtained by the Persian, Snow; compared with which, they acknowledged those of English cats had little brilliance, eclipsed, like the unimportant victories of the Howes, by the puissant Clinton and Arbuthnot, and the still more puissant Cornwallis. It sung that thou didst owe thy matchless might to thy lineal descent from the invincible Alexander, as he derived his more than mortal valour from his mother Olympia's illicit commerce with Jupiter. They sang that, amid the renowned siege of Persepolis, while Roxana and Statira were contending for the honour of his attentions, the conqueror of the world deigned to bestow them upon a large white female cat, thy grandmother, warlike Mr Snow, in the ten thousandth and ninety-ninth ascent.

Thus far their triumphant din was music to my ear; and even when it sung that lakes of milk ran curdling into whey, within the ebon conclave of their pancheons, with terror at thine approach; that mice squealed from all the neighbouring garrets; and that whole armies of Norway Rats, crying out amain, 'the devil take the hindmost', ran violently into the minster-pool, at the first gleam of thy white mail through the shrubs of Mr Howard's garden.

But O! when they sung, or rather yelled, of larks warbling on sunbeams, fascinated suddenly by the glare of thine eyes, and falling into thy remorseless talons; of robins, warbling soft and solitary upon the leafless branch, till the pale cheek of winter dimpled into joy; of hundreds of those bright-breasted songsters, torn from their barren sprays by thy pitiless fangs! – Alas! my heart died within me at the idea of so preposterous a union!

Marry you, Mr Snow, I am afraid I cannot; since, though the laws of our community might not oppose our connection, yet those of principle, of delicacy, of duty to my mistress, do very powerfully oppose it.

As to presiding at your concert, if you extremely wish it, I may perhaps grant your request; but then you must allow me to sing a song of my own composition, applicable to our present situation, and set to music by my sister Sophy at Mr Brown's the organist's, thus:

(Air: *Affettuoso*)

He, whom Pussy Po detains
A captive in her silken chains,
Must curb the furious thirst of prey,
Nor rend the warbler from his spray!
Nor let his wild, ungenerous rage
An unprotected foe engage.

146

O, should cat of Darwin prove
Foe to pity, foe to love!
Cat, that listens day by day,
To mercy's mild and honied lay,
Too surely would the dire disgrace
More deeply brand our future race,
The stigma fix, where'er they range,
That cats can ne'er their nature change.

Should I consent with thee to wed,
These sanguine crimes upon thy head,
And ere the wish'd reform I see,
Adieu to lapping Seward's tea!
Adieu to purring gentle praise
Charm'd as she quotes thy master's lays! –
Could I, alas! our kittens bring
Where sweet her plumy favourites sing,
Would not the watchful nymph espy
Their father's fierceness in their eye,

And drive us far and wide away,
In cold and lonely barn to stray?
Where the dark owl, with hideous scream,
Shall mock our yells for forfeit cream,
As on starv'd mice we swearing dine,
And grumble that our lives are nine.

Chorus (Largo)

Waal, woee, trone, moan, mall, oll, moule.

The still too much admired Mr Snow will have the
goodness to pardon the freedom of these expostulations,
and excuse their imperfections. The morning, O Snow!

147

had been devoted to this my correspondence with thee, but I was interrupted in that employment by the visit of two females of our species, who fed my ill-starved passion by praising thy wit and endowments, exemplified by thy elegant letter, to which the delicacy of my sentiments obliges me to send so inauspicious a reply.

I am, dear Mr Snow

Your ever obliged

Po Felina

The Yellow Terror

W. L. Alden

'Speaking of cats,' said Captain Foster, 'I'm free to say that I don't like 'em. I don't care to be looked down on by any person, whether he be man or cat. I know I ain't the President of the United States, nor yet a millionaire, nor yet the Boss of New York, but all the same I calculate that I'm a man, and entitled to be treated as such. Now, I never knew a cat yet that didn't look down on me, same as cats do on everybody. A cat considers that men are just dirt under his or her paws, as the case may be. I can't see what it is that makes a cat believe that he is so everlastingly superior to all the men that have ever lived, but there's no denying the fact that such is his belief, and he acts accordingly. There was a professor here one day, lecturing on all sorts of animals, and I asked him if he could explain this aggravating conduct of cats. He said that it was because cats used to be gods, thousands of years ago in the land of Egypt; but I didn't believe him. Egypt is a Scripture country, and consequently we ought not to believe anything about it that we don't read in the Bible. Show me anywhere in the Bible that Egyptian cats are mentioned as having practised as gods, and I'll believe it. Till you show it to me, I'll take the liberty of disbelieving any worldly statements that professors or anybody else may make about Egypt.

'The most notorious cat I ever met was old Captain Smedley's Yellow Terror. His real legal name was just plain Tom: but being yellow, and being a holy terror in many respects, it got to be the fashion among his acquaintances to call him the 'Yellow Terror'. He was a tremendous big cat, and he had been with Captain Smedley for five years before I saw him.

'Smedley was one of the best men I ever knew. I'll admit that he was a middling hard man on his sailors, so that his ship got the reputation of being a slaughterhouse, which it didn't really deserve. And there is no denying that he was a very religious man, which was another thing which made him unpopular with the men. I'm a religious man myself, even when I'm at sea, but I never held with serving out religion to a crew, and making them swallow it with belaying pins. That's what old Smedley used to do. He was in command of the barque *Medford*, out of Boston, when I knew him. I mean the city of Boston in Massachusetts, and not the little town that folks over in England call Boston: and I must say that I can't see why they should copy the names of our cities, no matter how celebrated they may be. Well! The *Medford* used to sail from Boston to London with grain, where she discharged her cargo and loaded again for China. On the outward passage we used to stop at Madeira, and the Cape, and generally Bangkok, and so on to Canton, where we filled up with tea, and then sailed for home direct.

'Now thishyer Yellow Terror had been on the ship's books for upwards of five years when I first met him. Smedley had him regularly shipped, and signed his name to the ship articles, and held a pen in his paw while he made a cross. You see, in those days the underwriters wouldn't let a ship go to sea without a cat, so as to keep the rats from getting at the cargo. I don't know what a land cat may do, but there ain't a seafaring cat that would look at a rat. What with the steward, and the cook and the men forrard being always ready to give the ship's cat a bite, the cat is generally full from kelson to deck, and wouldn't take the trouble to speak to a rat, unless one was to bite her tail. But, then, underwriters never know anything about what goes on at sea, and it's a shame that a sailorman should be compelled to give in to their ideas. The Yellow Terror had the general idea that the *Medford* was his private yacht, and that all hands were there to wait on him. And Smedley sort of confirmed him in that idea, by treating him with more respect than he treated his owners, when he was ashore. I don't blame the cat, and after I got to know what sort of a person the cat really was, I can't say as I blamed Smedley to any great extent.

'Tom, which I think I told you was the cat's real name, was far and away the best fighter of all cats in Europe, Asia, Africa and America. Whenever we sighted land he would get himself up in his best fur, spending hours brushing and polishing it, and biting his claws so as to make sure that they were as sharp as they could be made. As soon as the ship was made fast to the quay, or anchored in the harbour, the Yellow Terror went ashore to look for trouble. He always got it too, though he had such a reputation as a fighter, that whenever he showed himself, every cat that recognised him broke for cover. Why, the gatekeeper at the London Docks – I mean the one at the Shadwell entrance – told me that he always knew when the *Medford* was warping into dock, by the stream of cats that went out of the gate, as if a pack of hounds were after them. You see that as soon as the *Medford* was reported, and word passed among the cats belonging to the ships in dock that the Yellow Terror had

151

arrived, they judged that it was time for them to go ashore, and stop till the *Medford* should sail. Whitechapel used to be regularly overflowed with cats, and the newspapers used to have letters from scientific chaps trying to account for what they called the wave of cats that had spread over East London.

'I remember that once we laid alongside of a Russian brig, down in the basin by Old Gravel Lane. There was a tremendous big black cat sitting on the poop, and as soon as he caught sight of our Tom, he sung out to him, remarking that he was able and ready to wipe the deck up with him at any time. We all understood that the Russian was a new arrival who hadn't ever heard of the Yellow Terror, and we knew that he was, as the good book says, rushing on his fate. Tom was sitting on the rail near the mizzen rigging when the Russian made his remarks, and he didn't seem to hear them. But presently we saw him going slowly aloft till he reached our crossjack yard. He laid out on the yard arm till he was near enough to jump on to the mainyard of the Russian, and the first thing that the Russian cat knew Tom landed square on his back. The fight didn't last more than one round, and at the end of that, the remains of the Russian cat sneaked behind a water cask, and the Yellow Terror came back by the way of the crossjack yard and went on fur brushing, as if nothing had happened.

'When Tom went ashore in a foreign port he generally stopped ashore till we sailed. A few hours before we cast off hawsers, Tom would come aboard. He always knew when we were going to sail, and he never once got left. I remember one time when we were just getting up anchor in Cape Town harbour, and we all reckoned that this time we should have to sail without Tom, he having evidently stopped ashore just a little too long. But presently alongside comes a boat, with Tom lying back at full length in the sternsheets, for all the world like a drunken sailor who has been delaying the ship, and is proud of it. The boatman said that Tom had come down to the pier and jumped into his boat, knowing that the man would row him off to the ship, and calculating that Smedley would be glad to pay the damage. It's my belief that if Tom hadn't found a boatman, he would have chartered the government launch. He had the cheek to do that or anything else.

'Fighting was really Tom's only vice; and it could hardly be called a vice, seeing as he always licked the other cat, and hardly ever came out of a fight with a torn ear or a black eye. Smedley always said that Tom was religious. I used to think that was rubbish; but after I had been with Tom for a couple of voyages I began to believe what Smedley said about him. Every Sunday when the weather permitted, Smedley used to hold service on the quarter-deck. He was a Methodist, and when it came to ladling out Scripture, or singing a hymn, he could give odds to almost any preacher. All hands, except the man at the wheel, and the lookout, were required to attend service on Sunday morning, which naturally caused considerable grumbling, as the watch below considered they had a right to sleep in peace, instead of being dragged aft for service. But they had to knock under, and what they considered even worse, they had to sing, for the old man kept a bright lookout while the singing was going on, and if he caught any man malingering and not doing his full part of the singing he would have a few words to say to that man with a belaying pin, or a rope's end, after the service was over.

'Now Tom never failed to attend service, and to do his level best to help. He would sit somewhere near the old man and pay attention to what was going on better than I've seen some folks do in first-class churches ashore. When the men sang, Tom would start in and let out a yell here and there, which showed that he meant well even if he had never been to a singing-school, and didn't exactly understand singing according to Gunter. First along, I thought that it was all an accident that the cat came to service, and I calculated that his yelling during the singing meant that he didn't like it. But after a while I had to admit that Tom enjoyed the Sunday service as much as the Captain himself, and I agreed with Smedley that the cat was a thoroughgoing Methodist.

'Now after I'd been with Smedley for about six years, he got married all of a sudden. I didn't blame him, for in the first place it wasn't any of my business; and, in the next place, I hold that a ship's captain ought to have a wife, and the underwriters would be a sight wiser if they insisted that all captains should be married, instead of insisting that all ships should carry cats. You see that if a ship's captain has a wife, he is naturally anxious to get back to her, and have his best clothes mended, and his food cooked to suit him. Consequently he wants to make good passages and he don't want to run the risk of drowning himself, or of getting into trouble with his owners, and losing his berth. You'll find, if you look into it, that married captains live longer, and get on better than unmarried men, as it stands to reason that they ought to do.

'But it happened that the woman Smedley married was an Agonyostic, which is a sort of person that doesn't believe in anything, except the multiplication table, and such-like human vanities. She didn't lose any time in getting Smedley round to her way of thinking, and instead of being the religious man he used to be, he chucked the whole thing, and used to argue with me by the hour at a time, to prove that religion was a waste of time, and that he hadn't any soul, and had never been created, but had just descended from a family of seafaring monkeys. It made me sick to

154

hear a respectable sailorman talking such rubbish, but of course, seeing as he was my commanding officer, I had to be careful about contradicting him. I wouldn't ever yield an inch to his arguments, and I told him as respectfully as I could, that he was making the biggest mistake of his life. 'Why, look at the cat,' I used to say, 'he's got sense enough to be religious, and if you was to tell him that he was descended from a monkey, he'd consider himself insulted.' But it wasn't any use. Smedley was full of his new agonyostical theories, and the more I disagreed with him, the more set he was in his way.

'Of course he knocked off holding Sunday morning services; and the men ought to have been delighted, considering how they used to grumble at having to come aft and sing hymns, when they wanted to be below. But there is no accounting for sailors. They were actually disappointed when Sunday came and there wasn't any service. They said that we should have an unlucky voyage, and that the old man, now that he had got a rich wife, didn't consider sailors good enough to come aft on the quarter-deck, and take a hand in singing. Smedley didn't care for their opinion, but he was some considerable worried about the Yellow Terror. Tom missed the Sunday morning service, and he said so as plain as he could. Every Sunday, for three or four weeks, he came on deck, and took his usual seat near the captain, and waited for the service to begin. When he found out that there was no use in waiting for it, he showed that he disapproved of Smedley's conduct in the strongest way. He gave up being intimate with the old man, and once when Smedley tried to pat him, and be friendly, he swore at him, and bit him on the leg – not in an angry way, you understand, but just to show his disapproval of Smedley's irreligious conduct.

'When we got to London, Tom never once went

ashore, and he hadn't a single fight. He seemed to have lost all interest in worldly things. He'd sit on the poop in a melancholy sort of way, never minding how his fur looked, and never so much as answering if a strange cat sang out to him. After we left London he kept below most of the time, and finally, about the time that we were crossing the line, he took to his bed, as you might say, and got to be as thin and weak as if he had been living in the forecastle of a lime-juicer. And he was that melancholy that you couldn't get him to take an interest in anything. Smedley got to be so anxious about him that he read up in his medical book to try and find out what was the matter with him; and finally made up his mind that the cat had a first-class disease with a big name something like spinal menagerie. That was some little satisfaction to Smedley, but it didn't benefit the cat any; for nothing that Smedley could do would induce Tom to take medicine. He wouldn't so much as sniff at salts, and when Smedley tried to poultice his neck, he considered himself insulted, and roused up enough to take a piece out of the old man's ear.

'About that time we touched at Funchal, and Smedley sent ashore to lay in another tomcat, thinking that perhaps a fight would brace Tom up a little. But when the new cat was put down alongside of Tom, and swore at him in the most impudent sort of way, Tom just turned over on his other side, and pretended to go asleep. After that we all felt that the Yellow Terror was done for. Smedley sent the new cat ashore again, and told me that Tom was booked for the other world, and that there wouldn't be any more luck for us on that voyage.

'I went down to see the cat, and though he was thin and weak, I couldn't see any signs of serious disease about him. So I says to Smedley that I didn't believe the cat was sick at all.

'"Then what's the matter with him?" says the old man. "You saw yourself that he wouldn't fight, and when he's got to that point I consider that he is about done with this world and its joys and sorrows."

'"His nose is all right," said I. "When I felt it just now it was as cool as a teetotaller's."

'"That does look as if he hadn't any fever to speak of," says Smedley, "and the book says that if you've got spinal menagerie you're bound to have a fever."

'"The trouble with Tom," says I, 'is mental: that's what it is. He's got something on his mind that is wearing him out."

'"What can he have on his mind?" says the captain. "He's got everything to suit him aboard this ship. If he was a millionaire he couldn't be better fixed. He won all his fights while we were in Boston, and hasn't had a fight since, which shows that he can't be low-spirited on account of a licking. No, sir! You'll find that Tom's mind is all right."

'"Then what gives him such a mournful look out of his eyes?" says I. "When you spoke to him this morning he looked at you as if he was on the point of crying over your misfortunes – that is to say, if you've got any. Come to think of it, Tom begun to go into thishyer decline just after you were married. Perhaps that's what's the matter with him."

'But there was no convincing Smedley that Tom's trouble was mental, and he was so sure that the cat was going to die, that he got to be about as low-spirited as Tom himself. "I begin to wish," says Smedley to me one morning, "that I was a Methodist again, and believed in a hereafter. It does seem kind of hard that a first-class cat-fighter like Tom shouldn't have a chance when he dies. He was a good religious cat if ever there was

157

one, and I'd like to think that he was going to a better world."

'Just then an idea struck me. "Captain Smedley," says I, "you remember how Tom enjoyed the meetings that we used to have aboard here on Sunday mornings!"

'"He did so," said Smedley. "I never saw a person who took more pleasure in his Sunday privileges than Tom did."

'"Captain Smedley," says I, putting my hand on the old man's sleeve. "All that's the matter with Tom is seeing you deserting the religion that you was brought up in, and turning agonyostical, or whatever you call it. I call it turning plain infidel. Tom's mourning about your soul, and he's miserable because you don't have any more Sunday-morning meetings. I told you the trouble was mental, and now you know it is."

'"Mebbe you're right," says Smedley, taking what I'd said in a peaceable way, instead of flying into a rage, as I expected he would. "To tell you the truth, I ain't so well satisfied in my own mind as I used to be, and I was thinking last night, when I started in to say 'Now I lay me' – just from habit you know – that if I'd stuck to the Methodist persuasion I should be a blamed sight happier than I am now."

'"Tomorrow's Sunday," says I, "and if I was you, Captain, I should have the bell rung for service, same as you used to do, and bring Tom up on deck, and let him have the comfort of hearing the rippingest hymns you can lay your hand to. It can't hurt you, and it may do him a heap of good. Anyway, it's worth trying, if you really want the Yellow Terror to get well."

'"I don't mind saying," says Smedley, "that I'd do almost anything to save his life. He's been with me now going on for seven years, and we've never had a hard word. If a

Sunday-morning meeting will be any comfort to him, he shall have it. Mebbe if it doesn't cure him, it may sort of smooth his hatchway to the tomb."

'Now the very next day was Sunday, and at six the Captain had the bell rung for service, and the men were told to lay aft. The bell hadn't fairly stopped ringing, when Tom comes up the companionway, one step at a time, looking as if he was on his way to his own funeral. He came up to his usual place alongside of the capstan, and lay down on his side at the old man's feet, and sort of looked up at him with what anybody would have said was a grateful look. I could see that Smedley was feeling pretty serious. He understood what the cat wanted to say, and when he started in to give out a hymn, his voice sort of choked. It was a ripping good hymn, with a regular hurricane chorus, and the men sung it for all they were worth, hoping that it would meet Tom's views. He was too weak to join in with any of his old-time yells, but he sort of flopped the deck with his tail, and you could see he was enjoying it down to the ground.

'Well, the service went on just as it used to do in old times, and Smedley sort of warmed up as it went along, and by and by he'd got the regular old Methodist glow on his face. When it was all through, and the men had gone forrard again, Smedley stooped down, and picked up Tom, and kissed him, and the cat nestled up in the old man's neck and licked his chin. Smedley carried Tom down into the saloon, and sung out to the steward to bring some fresh meat. The cat turned to and ate as good a dinner as he'd ever eaten in his best days, and after he was through, he went into Smedley's own cabin, and curled up in the old man's bunk, and went to sleep purring fit to take the deck off. From that day Tom improved steadily, and by the time we got to Cape Town he was well enough to go ashore, though he was still considerable weak. I went ashore at the same time, and kept an eye on Tom, to see what he would do. I saw him pick out a small measly-looking cat, that couldn't have stood up to a full-grown mouse, and lick him in less than a minute. Then I knew that Tom was all right again, and I admired his judgment in picking out a small cat that was suited to his weak condition. By the time that we got to Canton, Tom was as well in body and mind as he had ever been; and when we sailed, he came aboard with two inches of his tail missing, and his starboard ear carried away, but he had the air of having licked all creation, which I don't doubt he had done, that is to say, so far as all creation could be found in Canton.

'I never heard any more of Smedley's agonyostical nonsense. He went back to the Methodists again, and he always said that Tom had been the blessed means of showing him the error of his ways. I heard that when he got back to Boston, he gave Mrs Smedley notice that he expected her to go to the Methodist meeting with him every Sunday, and that if she didn't, he should consider that it was a breach of wedding articles, and equivalent to mutiny. I don't know how she took it, or what the consequences were, for I left the *Medford* just then, and took command of a barque that traded between Boston and the West Indies. And I never heard of the Yellow Terror after that voyage, though I often thought of him, and always held that for a cat he was the ablest cat, afloat or ashore, that any man ever met.'

Cat in Church

Allen E. Woodall

The murmur of the service had begun.
Beyond the Saviour's robe and golden sheaves,
Glowing deep in the Sunday-morning sun,
Was the pagan voice of the sparrows in the eaves.
The choir subsided, the responses rose,
The prayer books fluttered idly to a close,
And a restless hush fell on the creaking pews,
When another pagan stepped along the aisle.
And, silent as any thought, a cat was there.
The congregation broke into a smile,
And something vibrant entered, like the air
From earthward portals. Feeling the gaze of all,
The cat cocked backed her small, self-conscious ears,
And fled with dignity along the wall,
A shadow of eager life from the endless years.

The White Mog

Ernest Dudley

(the 'Armchair Detective')

First time he saw it, he could hardly credit his luck.

Latish, autumn night it is, and Fred Ellis is on his usual prowl. Averaged him seven or eight cats a week it did – which at up to £20–30 a time couldn't be bad. He covered different parts of London, different nights of the week. Him and his little van. All the gear you needed was a little van. And a couple of sacks, of course.

So long as the mogs could breathe, okay. Might yowl and scratch, but no sweat. Needed a dead mog, you did, like a hole in the head. This white cat, it was a real beaut. He'd spotted it in the gardens from St Mary's Church in the square – its owners, he guessed, being the churchwarden and his wife, who lived next door to St Mary's – and even though it'd been only this brief flash, the white cat had made him drool at the thought of it in his sack.

He'd checked the time. Just gone eight thirty.

Next night he'd be there, same time. People mostly put their cats out at the same time every night. Later in the summer, of course.

So next night he's there. On the dot. And suddenly

there it is. In the light of the street lamp, it's all gleaming, brilliant white. Made your eyes pop, it was that white. And it looked even bigger. But, same as last time, it was there for only a couple of seconds. Then – nothing. Fred Ellis wondered what had made it take off like that. He cursed – then, suddenly again, there it was. A few yards further along the railings towards St Mary's wide steps. It was a bit misty, so perhaps it hadn't seen him.

He went after it, dead cautious, his sack in his left hand, held behind his back.

The cat was a moving white wraith, and something told Fred Ellis his luck was in as, stealthily, he followed it.

Then the white cat saw him. He stopped, hardly breathing. But it didn't take off. It stood there on the church steps, it did, thick furry tale flicking, eyes glowing greenish-gold. Then – would you believe it?—it was *purring* . . . purring an invitation to him! He was only a couple of yards away. It was the moment to pounce.

'Hello, white cat,' Fred Ellis said softly. Its pale, pinkish ears twitched. 'Come on, puss, we're pals, aint we?'

But then it turned and went up the steps to St Mary's big oak doors. For a moment a swirl of mist gave it a ghostly appearance, then it was there again and one of the great doors was slightly open. Fred Ellis could have laughed out loud – *the cat was about to enter the church.* It was locked at nine thirty. He'd once noticed the churchwarden locking it from inside. The churchwarden also locked the glass doors inside, leading to the nave and the altar beyond. So, once inside the big doors, the cat would be trapped in the space between them and the doors to the nave.

How he knew the layout of the church entrance was because one day he had helped an old girl with two sticks up the wide steps and through the glass doors to the nave. She had been profusely grateful, plus he'd managed to nick the small purse from her handbag – its lock was faulty, and it had been an open invitation. Inside there were only a couple of quid and some silver, but it was all grist to your mill. He'd returned the purse as he'd pushed the old dear into the nave.

The white cat went in, and Fred Ellis knew it was as good as his – he could feel it struggling in his sack. He sucked in his breath as the white furry tail disappeared and, letting out the air through his lips in a hiss, he dashed forward. He pulled the big door wide open and, slamming it behind him, reached for his pocket torch.

Then, he froze.

Dozens of pairs of greenish-gold eyes blazed at him in the darkness. His whole body crawled with terror. He spun round. But more eyes blazed at him. The place was alive with cats. He started for the door, but the eyes sprang, yowling, spitting. Cat's claws slashed his face and neck. He could feel the blood spurting. Dreadful claws tore his body.

He let out a frightful shriek as the cats ripped him. Shriek after shriek.

The agonised shrieks reached Dr Havers and his wife who were passing by and they dashed up the steps, pulled the big door open, found the light switch and, in the glare, saw Fred Ellis sprawled on the floor, one hand gripping his sack, the other, which had held the torch but dropped it, outstretched.

Dr Havers bent and felt his pulse. As he straightened up, shaking his head, his wife asked, 'What was all that about?'

'Must have had a heart-attack,' Dr Havers said. He glanced round. A non-committal shrug. Stared down. There wasn't a mark on Fred Ellis's face. Not a mark of a hundred slashing claws, tearing his face to pieces.

Not a mark.

The Miracle of St Simon's

Marian Evans

On Cornwall's rugged coastline bare,
A steeple scythed into the air
Above a fishing village scene
That time had frozen, like a dream;
The cobbled streets, the hedgerow flowers,
St Simon's chimes that marked the hours.
Inside a cat slept on a pew,
In stained-glass sunlight, red and blue

And when the fleet brought in its catch
At dawn old puss would sit and watch
As on the quay the herring writhed
Beneath the fishwives' flashing knives.
Yet never once, the sailors learned,
Did the cat steal what he'd not earned.
He only ate, inside God's house,
The vicar's scraps or heathen mouse.

The seasons passed, the years went by,
But still the cat went to the quay.
Then one fine day the village folk
Decided all their fish to smoke,

And so beside the church they raised
A smokehouse, which the vicar praised.
But as the building reached its height
None noticed how it blocked the light.

Outside the church the smokehouse grew
Until the stained glass, red and blue,
No longer shed its saintly glow
Upon the cat asleep below.
One day at dusk a builder's pole
Fell on the glass and made a hole,
At this the cat took great affright
And disappeared into the night.

It wasn't till a week had passed
That the church cat returned at last:
Bedraggled now he turned away
All proffered food, and scorned the quay.
The vicar tried his best to cheer
But all now knew his end was near.
Only a miracle, they said,
Could prevent him soon from being dead.

In penance for their carelessness
The workmen tidied up the mess
And on the sill installed a mat
Of softest velvet for the cat
So that through the clear-glass plate
He could see out and meditate
On life's short span and Heaven's throne
Which countless souls like his have known.

Another sight which caught his eye
Were seagulls by the smokery,

But ever at the close of day
The squealing birds all flew away.
Intrigued, one day the cat crept down
And weakly crossed the hallowed ground
Until he reached the herring shed
And gingerly stuck round his head . . .

High above on wires of steel
Hung row on row of fishy meal.
Temptation racked him like a fever,
But the cat knew he could never
Take what belonged to other men
And so he turned away, but then
A kipper fell right at his feet
And, startled, he began to eat.

When he had finished half the flesh
A dozen fish fell with a crash.
The cat then rushed out of the door
As snapped wires tossed down dozens more.
His strength returned, he then raced,
Back through the churchyard to the place
By the window whence he came
Just as the smoke-house burst in flame.

The vicar, working late that night,
Was filled with joy at the glad sight
Of his cat running down the aisle
And stroked the tabby with a smile.
The cat, slipping his fingers through,
Leapt to the window, red and blue.
The priest then saw all was not well
Through the clear pane and rang the bell.

The villagers rushed up the hill,
Leaving their boats and evening meal,
But though the firemen crowded round
The smokehouse burnt down to the ground.
A miracle, declared the people,
Had saved their church and its steeple
Which, the guidebooks all agreed,
Was a holy treasure indeed.

As the fisherfolk knelt to pray
To thank their God for this good day,
The vicar blessed the old church cat
And praised the Lord in Heaven that
His pious fast had brought no harm
For without the cat the alarm
Would not have rung in loud, long notes
And brought them quickly from their boats.

The inquest found after some days
What had caused the smokehouse blaze:
The kippers falling from their wire
Upset a lamp and caused a fire.
When the insurance was all paid
A brand new smokehouse then was made,
Far away in a sheltered pass
And excess funds bought new stained glass.

So now our tale is almost done
Of a brave cat and honour won.
Above that rugged coastline bare
A steeple scythes yet in the air;
St Simon's chimes still mark the hours
O'er cobbled streets and hedgerow flowers;
A cat once more sleeps on a pew
In stained-glass sunlight, red and blue.

The Best Bed

Sylvia Townsend Warner

The cat had known many winters, but none like this. Through two slow darkening months it had rained, and now, on the eve of Christmas, the wind had gone round to the east, and instead of rain, sleet and hail fell.

The hard pellets hit his drenched sides and bruised them. He ran faster. When boys threw stones at him he could escape by running; but from this heavenly lapidation there was no escape. He was hungry, for he had had no food since he had happened upon a dead sparrow, dead of cold, three days ago. It had not been the cat's habit to eat dead meat, but having fallen upon evil days he had been thankful even for that unhealthy-tasting flesh. Thirst tormented him, worse than hunger. Every now and then he would stop, and scrape the frozen gutters with his tongue. He had given up all hope now, he had forgotten all his wiles. He despaired, and ran on.

The lights, the footsteps on the pavements, the crashing buses, the swift cars like monster cats whose eyes could outstare his own, daunted him. Though a Londoner, he was not used to these things, for he was born by Thames-side, and had spent his days among the docks, a modest useful life of rat-catching and secure slumbers upon flour

171

sacks. But one night the wharf where he lived had caught fire; and terrified by flames, and smoke, and uproar, he had begun to run, till by the morning he was far from the river, and homeless, and too unversed in the ways of the world to find himself another home.

A street door opened, and he flinched aside, and turned a corner. But in that street, doors were opening too, every door letting out horror. For it was closing-time. Once, earlier in his wanderings, he had crouched by such a door, thinking that any shelter would be better than the rainy street. Before he had time to escape, a hand snatched him up and a voice shouted above his head. 'Gorblime if the cat hasn't come in for a drink,' the voice said. And the cat felt his nose thrust into a puddle of something fiery and stinking, that burned on in his nostrils and eyes for hours afterwards.

He flattened himself against the wall, and lay motionless until the last door should have swung open for the last time. Only when someone walked by, bearing that smell with him, did the cat stir. Then his nose quivered with invincible disgust, his large ears pressed back upon his head, and the tip of his tail beat stiffly upon the pavement. A dog, with its faculty of conscious despair, would have abandoned itself, and lain down to await death; but when the streets were quiet once more the cat ran on.

There had been a time when he ran and leaped for the pleasure of the thing, rejoicing in his strength like an athlete. The resources of that lean, sinewy body, disciplined in the hunting days of his youth, had served him well in the first days of his wandering; then, speeding before some barking terrier, he had hugged amidst his terrors a compact and haughty joy in the knowledge that he could so surely outstrip the pursuer; but now his strength would only serve to prolong his torment. Though an accumulated fatigue smouldered in every nerve, the obdurate limbs carried him on, and would carry him on still, a captive to himself, meekly trotting to the place of his death.

He ran as the wind directed, turning this way and that to avoid the gusts, spiked with hail, that ravened through the streets. His eyes were closed, but suddenly at a familiar sound he stopped, and stiffened with fear. It was the sound of a door swinging on its hinges. He snuffed apprehensively. There was a smell, puffed out with every swinging to of the door, but it was not the smell he abhorred and though he waited in the shadow of a buttress, no sounds of jangling voices came to confirm his fears, and though the door continued to open and shut, no footsteps came from it. He stepped cautiously from his buttress into a porch. The smell was stronger here. It was aromatic, rich and a little smoky. It tickled his nose and made him sneeze.

The door was swinging with the wind. The aperture was small, too small for anything to be seen through it, save only a darkness that was not quite dark. With a sudden determination the cat flitted through.

Of his first sensations, one overpowered all the others. Warmth! It poured over him, it penetrated his being, and confused his angular physical consciousness of cold and hunger and fatigue into something rounded and indistinct. Half-swooning, he sank down on the stone flags.

Another sneezing fit roused him. He jumped up, and began to explore.

The building he was in reminded him of home. Often, hunting the riverside, he had strayed into places like this – lofty and dusky, stone-floored and securely uninhabited. But they had smelt of corn, of linseed, of tallow, of sugar: none of them had smelt as this did, smokily sweet. They had been cold. Here it was warm. They had been dark; and here the dusk was mellowed with one red star, burning in mid-air, and with the glimmer of a few tapers, that added to the smoky sweetness their smell of warm wax.

His curiosity growing with his confidence, the cat ran eagerly about the church. He rubbed his back against the font, he examined into the varying smell of the hassocks, he trotted up the pulpit stairs, sprang on to the ledge, and sharpened his claws in the cushion. Outside the wind boomed, and the hail clattered against the windows, but within the air was warm and still, and the red star burned mildly on. Over against the pulpit the cat came on something that reminded him even more of home – a wisp of hay, lying on the flags. He had often seen hay; sometimes borne towering above the greasy tide on barges, sometimes fallen from the nosebags of the great draught horses who waited so peacefully in the wharfingers' yard.

The hay seemed to have fallen from a box on trestles, cut out of unstained wood. The cat stood on his hind legs, and tried to look in, but it was too high for him. He turned about, but his curiosity brought him back again; and poising himself on his clustered paws he rocked slightly, gauging his spring, and then jumped, alighting softly in a bed of hay. He landed so delicately that though the two kneeling figures at either end of the crib swayed forward for a moment, they did not topple over. The cat sniffed them, a trifle suspiciously, but they did not hold his attention long. It was the hay that interested him. A drowsy scent rose out of the deep, warm bed as he kneaded and shuffled it with his fore-paws. This, this, promised him what he had so long yearned for: sound sleep, an enfolding in warmth and softness, a nourishing forgetfulness. He paced round in a small circle, burrowing himself a close nest, purring with a harsh note of joy. As he turned he brushed against a third figure in the crib; but he scarcely noticed it. Already a rapture of sleepiness was overcoming him; the two kneeling figures had done him no harm, nor would this reposing one. Soon the bed was made to his measure. Bowing his head upon his paws, he abandoned himself.

Another onslaught of hail dashed against the windows, the door creaked, and at a gust of wind entering the church the candle flames wavered, as though they were nodding their heads in assent; but though the cat's ears flicked once or twice against the feet of the plaster Jesus, he was too securely asleep to know or heed.

Acknowledgments

Arnold Bennett, 'The Cat and Cupid' from *The Matador of the Five Towns*, reprinted by permission of A. P. Watt Ltd on behalf of Mme V. M. Eldin

George Mackay Brown, 'The Cure' from *Six Lives of Fankle the Cat*, reprinted by permission of John Murray (Publishers) Ltd

Ernest Dudley, 'The White Mog', reprinted by permission of the author

Marian Evans, 'The Miracle of St Simon's', reprinted by permission of the author

S. J. Forrest, 'Cat Cult' from *Saints & Synods*, reprinted by permission of Mowbray Ltd

Geoffrey Household, 'Abner of the Porch' from *The Europe That was*, reprinted by permission of A. M. Heath Ltd

M. R. James, 'The Stalls of Barchester Cathedral' from *Collected Ghost Stories*, reprinted by permission of N. J. R. James on behalf of the Estate of M. R. James

Bryan MacMahon, 'The Cat in the Cornfield' from *The Red Petticoat and Other Stories*, reprinted by permission of Macmillan Ltd

Christopher Park, 'The Case of the Cross-eyed Sphinx and the Holy Ghost', reprinted by permission of the author